I Kille
So She Can
Live

Tamika Ingram

THE
Vision to Fruition
GROUP
PUBLISHING INVESTING CONSULTING ACADEMY

I Killed Her So She Can Live

ISBN: 978-0-578-72626-7

Library of Congress Control Number: 2020914548

Cover Photo by The Vision to Fruition Group
Editing and Layout by LCB Consulting and Design
www.consultLatricia.com

The Vision to Fruition Publishing House
www.vision-fruition.com

Dedication

I wrote this book in faith that through my transparency all of you will be able to die to yourselves.

This book is dedicated to all of the kings and queens across the globe that have had to fight with themselves in order to take control of their lives and shape their future to the desires they have always dreamed of. I declare and decree that when you finish reading this book in its entirety, your lives will never be the same and that God will do exceedingly, abundantly and above all you could ever ask or think.

Acknowledgements

Writing a book is more tedious than I thought. It is more than typing up words on a page. This book has stretched me beyond my limits and made me realize that I can achieve anything I put my mind to do. God has graced me to share my story with the world, and I thank Him for giving me the strength, the confidence, and the words to type that will change lives.

I must start off by acknowledging my son. You checked on me every night. You were the very first person to hold my hand and pray that this book will be a #1 best seller. Your prayers, hugs, kisses, and powerful words are what got me through the most tiring and exhausting hours. Words cannot express the joy I have in my heart to have you for a son. I love you.

I am eternally grateful for Tia Ingram, who inspired and motivated me to write this book to completion. Thank you for your encouraging words every time I wanted to quit. There were countless times I had writer's block and wanted to throw in the towel. Thank you for holding me accountable and pushing me past my comfort zone. I also want to thank you for the late nights you sacrificed your sleep to proofread some of the chapters for the reassurance I needed. None of this would be possible if it were not for your patience and support throughout this entire process. It is an honor to have you as my best friend.

A special thanks goes to Jasma Williams for coming over to my house to read the first couple of chapters the moment I asked. Thank you so much for taking the time to come over as soon as I called you. You could have refused or simply made me wait, but you did not hesitate to come over. I am forever grateful for your friendship, genuine love, and support.

Writing a book about my life was not the easiest since I had to involve my parents. I want to acknowledge my mother, Frances Marshall. Thank you for your love and support by allowing me to tell my truth freely without judging me. Thank you dearly for allowing me to interrupt your space at any given time for your feedback.

To my little sister, Tonni Gardner, who has always been my number one fan, your uplifting words meant the world to me. You snatched my laptop and could not stop reading. Watching your response gave me all the reassurance I needed to keep going. I love you.

I acknowledge my big brother, Travis Gardner. Thank you for listening when I needed you during the most difficult moments of writing my truth. You are an amazing big brother.

Finally, thank you to everyone involved in my getting my story published at The Vision to Fruition Publishing House. Thank you LaKesha Williams for allowing me the opportunity to share my story with the entire world. You have a heart of gold and I honor you for your love and patience. Thank you for allowing me to use your platform to reach the lives of millions.

Contents

Introduction

One of the HARDEST things to do in life is LETTING GO. It is hard to let go of the life we have been living. It is difficult letting go of the things the flesh loves, craves, and is accustomed to. Releasing people, pain, unforgiveness, bitterness, insecurities, low self-esteem, poverty, and a victim mentality are tough tasks. We would rather let these things slowly suffocate us and trap us rather than save our own lives. Self-love can be a dangerous obsession when you love the cravings of your flesh versus the cravings of your spirit. We pay less attention to our spirit—that will live for eternity—and more attention to our flesh, that is short-lived. In fact, many of us have become so infatuated with ourselves without realizing this means we have intense, but short-lived passion or admiration for someone or something. Our time on earth is short, and it is easy to live life as if it is guaranteed to last forever.

It is easy to let life's experiences, challenges, and obstacles place you in bondage wanting a way of escape but afraid to simply open the door to your freedom. I am writing this book for every King and Queen that feels trapped inside of themselves in desperate need of a way out. In this book, you will read about my personal life experiences suffocating from hurt, low self-esteem, baggage, marriage, lesbianism, unforgiveness, deceit, anger, and guilt. You will read about the choice I was forced to make and after reading this book you will have to decide. Can you picture yourself killing the one person you love the most? The person that you love to satisfy. The person that you wake up to every morning and sleep with every night. The person that you protect. The person that you depend on, lean on, and rely on for everything? I had to make one of two choices: (1) Be killed or (2) Kill to survive.

One: The Seed of Hurt

I ran full speed back into the house from the bus stop shouting,

"MA! MAAAAA! *The chaser cat* is outside!*"* I yelled while trying
to catch my breath.

"What's outside?" My mom replied in a very flummoxed tone.

"*THE CHASER CAT*! You know the cat that looks evil and is
always chasing animals up the tree to eat them. There is *NO* way I'm
going back out there!"

My mom started giggling.

"You really ought to be ashamed of yourself the way you carry on
about those cats! I'll just take you to school."

Living in Sylvester Georgia was the worst decision my mom ever made. My mother's name is Tonette, and she takes her relationship with Jesus very seriously. I believe she would sit on a throne next to Him if she could. My mother decided to marry a tall, dark-skinned, and lanky country bumpkin by the name of Drayton. Looking at him, I figured she married him solely because he was into church since he was not the finest. However, that was her man, so we had to move from the city of Columbus to the country with all the wild looking animals, weird looking creatures, dirt roads, woods, no street lights and a forty five minute drive if you wanted to go to the store or a fast food restaurant! We lived in a cozy, three-bedroom trailer in the middle of nowhere right across from all the woods. What a beautiful view! I thought sarcastically.

At the age of eleven, I had to learn how to adapt to a new middle school, a new living environment, new siblings, and a stepdad. Adjusting to a new school was not too bad because one of my older siblings, Tina, went to school with me. Tina was short and petite with long Indian hair. She was a freshman in high school. The difference between schools in the city and schools in the country was that they combined middle and high together, so that was a major plus for me.

Tina always walked the halls with me and waited for me after school. I could never understand the way country people talked. After school when I got on the bus, the driver said, "I will not pull off until everybody sit bike."

I thought, "Sit what?! Who's bike?" Completely confused, I asked Tina, "Who's bike is he talking about?"

Tina chuckled. "He's saying sit back not sit bike!"

"Ohhhh ok," I said, shaking my head and thinking to myself, "Lord have mercy, now I have to interpret the country grammar! Great job for this one Mother!"

When I got home from school, I would go straight to my room to do my homework, read some books, and do a couple of crossword puzzles. Playing outside in the wild was not an option for me. My oldest stepsister is Don. She was in her twenties, very loving, tall, and brown-skinned with curly hair. Every day she would help me pick out my school clothes. We laughed together a lot and watched TV together. We connected instantly, and I felt like she was my biological sister.

Having a stepdad was not too bad. Drayton was always to himself and serious about the Lord. He made us go to church every time the doors opened. We were not allowed to stay home. Church lasted for *hours*. Drayton would be shouting and running laps around the church. Tina and I would be sitting on the back row nodding off behind the fan held up to our face. We would jump every time we heard him shout. "Hallelujah!"

One Sunday evening after church Drayton, my mother and I went over to his brother's house for dinner. Tina was over her cousin's house for the weekend. It was very cold outside. I could hear the whistling of the wind as the cool breeze swept past my face. There were no streetlights, so it was easy to see all the wild animals hidden in the woods by the yellow beam that glowed from their eyes. It was a school night, and my mother was in a counseling session. She asked her Drayton to take me home so that I could prepare for school the following

> Fear gripped me from the inside out because I had never experienced such a romantic touch from an adult.

morning. While walking towards the car, I saw several bobcats in the woods. I began to walk faster so I could hurry up and jump in the car.

"Put on your seatbelt." Drayton said calmly.

As I reached over to fasten my seat belt, I felt a warm hand touch my thigh. Feeling uneasy, I did not say anything because I was unaware of the motive behind the touch. The touch then turned into a gentle caressing of my leg. Fear gripped me from the inside out because I had never experienced such a romantic touch from an adult. Riding silently and looking out of the window, I politely grabbed his hand and placed it back on his leg.

As we pulled up into the yard of our home, I opened the door and got out before Drayton could put the car in park. I went straight to my room and closed the door. In walks Drayton with a bottle of medicine in one hand and a silver spoon in the other.

"Take this so that you won't catch a cold," he said as he walked towards me.

"I feel fine. I don't need to take any medicine." I said brushing past him to walk out of my room.

Drayton grabbed me, picked me up and sat me in between his legs. He moaned while moving me around on his penis, and I could feel it get hard. The moment I realized what was happening, I tried to wiggle my way out of his arms, but I was not strong enough to escape his strong grip around my waist. Every time I would try to get away, he would grab me and slam me back down on his lap.

"LET ME GO!" I yelled.

He began to twist the top off the bottle of medicine.

"Dad!" Don shouted as she came through the front door.

Drayton immediately jumped up and walked out of my room.

Terrified and afraid, I hurried to close my door and lock it. Sliding to the ground, I broke down in tears. All I wanted was my mother, but she was not home to save me from the nightmare I had experienced. I remembered the words my mother would always say to me,

"You tell me everything. Don't ever keep me in the dark about anything."

Tears began to drench my cheeks like a waterfall. Picking up a pen and paper, I started writing my mother a letter telling her everything that happened, because I was too shook up to get any words out. With tears dripping all over the paper, feeling alone, afraid and hurting inside, I replayed the scene over and over and my cry became more intense. When the letter was complete, I folded the letter, and I sat by the door waiting for my mother to come home and check on me. I held the letter close and cried myself to sleep.

When my mother came home, she knocked on my door. I jumped up and opened the door handing her the letter immediately. My mother did not say a word. She sat down on my bed and started reading the letter. After she read the letter she said in a very frustrated and furious tone,

"Demonstrate everything that happened!".

After I demonstrated everything that happened my mother embraced me, apologized, and held me tight letting me know that I was safe assuring me that would never happen again. She walked out of my room and said,

"I'll be back."

Moments later she came back, and we laid together on the sofa. My mother cuddled me without letting go the entire night.

The next morning, my mom looked into my eyes,

"Now let's keep this between us. Do not tell your father nor your brother because they will hurt Drayton and end up in prison. Now, go pack all of your things we are leaving and never returning."

"Yes ma'am," I sighed feeling relieved. There is nothing like having a mom to take immediate action after a traumatic experience. She could have stayed. She could have believed him over me. Instead, my mother had my back, and from that moment on I grew an even closer bond and a deeper love for my mother.

Nervously, I started packing all my things and taking them to my mother's car hoping that we would finish before Drayton returned and caught us. After everything was packed, we got in the car and my mom said that she was about to go withdraw me from school. Riding down the road for about thirty minutes, I noticed my mom turning around going back towards the trailer.

"Why are we turning around?" I asked.

"I forgot to get my seasonings, juices and all the meat I just bought. I am not leaving him with anything of mine."

As I stared at her in total shock, I was

> Please Lord, don't let us die trying to rescue groceries.

completely lost for words. In my head I thought, this lady is turning all the way around risking our lives for some groceries! Did she forget that we are on the run? I shook my head and mumbled under my breath *Please Lord don't let us die trying to rescue groceries.*

As we pulled into the yard of the trailer, my mom hopped out of the car expeditiously.

"I'll be right back. Lock the doors," She said.

I sat in the car shaking like a leaf on a tree. I was so afraid. I was looking around nervously making sure Drayton didn't pull up.

"Please Lord let her hurry up," I whispered, bending down to tie my shoe. As soon as I looked up, there was Drayton's long, black, dusty Lincoln coming up the dirt road. I began to panic, and I unlocked the door to go get my mom out of the house, but she came out just in time carrying three trash bags full of groceries.

"Ma! Let's go! He's coming!" I shouted.

My mom got in the car, and we drove off passing him as he was pulling up into the yard. Moments later, I looked in the rear-view mirror and realized that Drayton was right behind us.

"Ma! He's behind us!" I gasped.

My mother immediately started praying and speaking in tongues. Rolling my eyes and turning towards the window I said in a low tone, "Now you wanna pray!"

At this point, I was feeling like we were on an episode of *C.O.P.S.* in a high-speed chase.

"This can't be real life," I said while looking up trying to keep the tears from falling.

Glancing over at my mother, she was driving calmly to the school as if we were not being followed. When we pulled up to the school, my mother got out of the car. I noticed Drayton was walking toward her. I was unable to hear their discussion, but I saw Drayton turn around and get back into his car and drive off. I guess speaking in tongues and prayer really works! My mother withdrew me from school, and we went back to the city never looking back.

I was excited that my mother rescued me, but I was deeply wounded from the thought of almost being raped, and I didn't know how to cope with it. As a child, I could not fathom what would make a man want an eleven-year-old girl. What if Don had never come home that night? My view of God changed. If he is so great, why did he let a grown man come on to me? Enjoying life as a normal eleven-year-old girl was difficult for me. The innocent joy I had faded. I told myself to never trust another male. I buried the hurt and pretended to be okay to be happy, because I didn't want my mother to think I was holding it against her.

In my teenage years, I spent a lot of time over my father and stepmother's house on weekends and summers. My father, Dennis, is controlling, silly and overly dramatic—over the top about everything.

His voice is stern like a drill sergeant and living with him was like being in the military.

"Mika! Mika!" He said one morning while turning on the light. I laid there silently with my eyes closed hoping he would walk away and come back later.

"Mika! I know you hear me!" He said while standing in the door. I realized he would not walk away unless I responded, "Sir?"

"What's on your itinerary today"? He asked.

I rolled over to look at the time on my cell phone. "Daddy it's 7 a.m. I don't know yet."

My dad commanded, "Well you need to be getting ready to get up. The living room needs to be vacuumed, and I'm sure it's some clothes that need to be folded."

"I just vacuumed the floor yesterday," I recalled.

"So, what," He argued. "Today is a new day and y'all need to clean up this damn room. It's nasty as hell." He turned off the light and walked away. There were only a juice box and a bag of chips on the nightstand.

My stepmother, Jessica, is extremely negative, rude and loves to gossip. There were plenty of times I overheard her talking about me to my dad. I never understood why she did not like me because I had not ever disrespected her. Every day I took pride in taking care of my little sisters. I would always make sure they ate, were well-dressed and I had their hair done before going outside. Jessica would always come home from work and re-do my stepsister Olivia's hair.

"Olivia come here let me do your hair. I'on like that bullshit. What kinda style that is?" I heard her say. She would re -do the exact same hairstyle I did.

One time, I fried some chicken and I offered her some and she declined. My dad ate some and said it was delicious.

"Well since it's so good, that's who you get to make your chicken from now on." Jessica said unpleasantly.

I never said anything. It hurt the most because my daddy never stood up for me as his daughter. He would let her say whatever she wanted to say to me and about me. Over the years, it got worse and I started feeling uncomfortable being around them. I knew her love for me was not genuine, and the hurt I felt inside turned into built up anger towards them both.

Two: Tampered Identity

After graduating high school in 2008, I started college, got a job in healthcare, and started attending church. The church had a small membership and could not afford a building. Every Sunday we had church in the conference room of a hotel. One Sunday, I was teaching in kids' ministry and I wanted to play a trivia game for prizes. I walked up to the front counter to purchase some candy and there stood this 5'10 light-skinned, tall, handsome man whose dress game was immaculate!

"Hey Love, I'm Dwayne, how may I assist you?" He said to me in a deep smooth tone. The tone of his voice melted my soul instantly like the sun beaming on chocolate.

"I would like to buy some candy please." I stood at the counter blushing.

"Pick out the candy you would like and it's on me," he said smoothly.

I picked out the candy of my preference, said thank you, and walked away. The whole time I was teaching the kids, in the back of my mind I was thinking about Dwayne.

After church service, I walked back to the counter and started conversing with him, and from there we exchanged numbers. Days later we started dating and I thought he was right for me. As time passed the relationship started to consist of him only wanting sex. I thought about Drayton wanting sex from me when I was eleven years old. Why is that all men see me as?

One night I stopped by his place after work. We spent time together and then he left the house. I waited up for him until I dozed off to sleep. When I woke up, I realized that he never came back. I tried calling him. An automated voice said, "The number you are calling is no longer in service. Message 4-0-3-4."

"This can't be right. Let me try again," I insisted. This time, I dialed his number out to make sure I was calling the right person.

"The number you are calling is...." I hung up, grabbed my things, and left his house. Minutes turned to hours. Hours turned into days and days turned into weeks without hearing from him. I would drive by his house and his car was never there.

I was driving to work when reality finally hit me. "Wow! This nigga really up and left me in his crib after sex, changed his number and moved!"

What Dwayne did was foul. I felt so stupid for hoping he would appreciate a loyal woman and see me beyond my physical

> The relationship started to consist of him only wanting sex. . ... Why is that all men see me as?

appearance. Every time I thought about how everything blew up in my face, the angrier I got.

"DAMN, NIGGAS AIN'T SHIT!" I yelled, hitting the steering wheel.

When I got to work, I received a text message from my high school sweetheart Michael. Michael was very loving but very insecure. We broke up after high school and he went off into the military. The message said, *"I'm in town and I would like to see you."* I was open to meeting him to mask the betrayal and anger I felt from Dwayne.

"Okay, I'm off this weekend," I texted.

Saturday morning, I woke up excited to meet Michael, but I did not want to seem desperate, so I waited until the afternoon to send a confirmation text about meeting him. I had to get my nails done and my eyebrows waxed because I wanted him to be speechless and drooling at my beauty.

We met at *Buffalo Wild Wings.* He met me at the door smiling from ear to ear.

"You're so beautiful. How have you been?" He smiled, welcoming me into his arms.

"I've been amazing," I said flirtatiously. We sat and talked for hours laughing and gazing into each other's eyes. Sealing the night with a soft goodnight kiss.

After dating awhile, we decided to build a solid relationship. The following month, I missed my cycle and decided to take a pregnancy test. The moment I looked at the positive results, I called to schedule an appointment with my OBGYN. When I got to the doctor's office, she called me to the back and performed a regular pap smear.

"Your cervix is blue," Dr. Karen said.

"What does that mean?" I was startled.

"You're definitely pregnant!" Dr. Karen responded.

I closed my eyes and started rubbing my face. Lying there, all I could think about was a baby growing inside of me. The thought of being pregnant was disappointing, because I was not financially prepared to be a mother. I thought about being pregnant and decided that I would secretly have an abortion. I called several clinics for the price of the procedure and health information.

One evening my mother's friend, Evangelist Michelle, came over to converse with my mom and play a game of *Skip Bo*, a sequencing card game. I enjoyed playing cards with Michelle because she loved to talk trash the whole game.

"You need to be taking notes, because I can't be stopped baby!" She said slamming the cards on the table.

"Baby all I got is that smoke ova' here!"

I didn't have a winning card in my hand. Before Michelle left, she said to me,

"The Holy Spirit is leading me to pray over you. Lift your hands."

Sitting at the dining room table, I began to lift my hands.

"The Lord said give birth to your baby. Do not have an abortion."

Tears filled my eyes instantly because I never told anyone my plan to have an abortion. I knew that was God speaking to me, and I cried for the remainder of the night. Nine months later, I gave birth to a healthy baby boy named Lamar. Michael and I decided to get married, raise our son and live happily ever after.

Eight months later, things took a turn for the worse quickly. The stress of trying to be a wife, work a full-time job and be a mom with no freedom at nineteen years old became overwhelming. Michael was stationed in Japan. The thirteen-hour time difference made it extremely difficult to be available for him when he needed me, and that caused a lot of arguments. He constantly accused me of cheating, and I got tired of arguing about all the times I cheated on him in high school. Yes, I was a player, but why must we keep discussing our teenage years? I thought. The arguments turned into continual verbal abuse and over time I became very nonchalant toward his feelings. In a heated argument he said,

"Let's just get a divorce."

"Ok, Send the papers!" I declared and hung up the phone. I was over it.

Needing a break from life, I decided to call my friend Denise to go out and have drinks with me. I arrived at Denise's house, and she let me in.

"I'll be dressed in 10 minutes!" she shouted as she rushed back up the stairs.

As I walked into the living room, I noticed there was a beautiful woman dressed weirdly standing beside the T.V. texting on her phone. She was wearing big shorts like she was borrowing them from her big brother, a *Nike* shirt, Jordans, and a fitted cap. I was looking for her boobs because I wasn't certain she was a woman. The more I looked, I noticed they were smashed down into one long breast. I didn't want to get caught staring at her, so I spoke reluctantly.

"Hey, how are you? I'm Tamika." she looked up and said,

"Hey, I'm fine. You can call me Danielle."

"Are you coming out with us tonight?" I asked.

"Us?" She laughed. "I didn't know you were coming."

"Same here." I replied.

That broke the ice between us, and we began to make small talk. Denise came downstairs, and the three of us went out for drinks.

Danielle and I exchanged numbers that night and conversed with one another every day after.

We talked about everything under the sun. She told me about her same-sex attraction. That explained why she dressed like a man or the proper term called, *stud*. I was completely oblivious to the whole LGBTQ+ lifestyle, but was curious. I learned that I was behind the curve ball and lesbianism is a popular thing. Danielle and I hung out every single day. Our bond grew stronger and we became best friends. In her presence, I felt the happiest I have ever felt in a long time. Being with her, I was getting the love, attention, and appreciation I have never received from any male. There was never a dull moment and I wanted to be around her all the time.

On a Thursday evening we decided to go bowling. We

"Tamika . . .This isn't what you want. What about Michael?" she asked. "We are getting a divorce."

were having a blast singing, eating, laughing, and cracking jokes. Danielle made me feel so comfortable around her. Afraid of losing her to someone else, I decided to come on to her. My turn came to bowl. After I bowled my ball down the lane, I sat on her lap and kissed her.

"Tamika, what are you doing? This isn't what you want." She looked into my eyes.

"What if it is what I want"? I pleaded.

"What about Michael?" she asked.

"We are getting a divorce," I said.

A couple of months later, Danielle and I became a couple and moved in together. We were so elated we went apartment shopping and out to dinner to celebrate. On our way to Cheddars, the restaurant, as we were pulling up to the red light, Danielle noticed a man in the lane beside us driving a smoke gray F-150 signaling us to roll down the window. He looked like he was in his late forties. Danielle rolled down her window to see what he wanted.

"Hey, I'm Jimmy! Y'all are some gorgeous women. Let me take y'all out tonight."

"Thank you," said Danielle.

"Take us where?" I shouted over Danielle.

"Write my number down," Jimmy said.

Danielle took her phone out pretending she was keying in the number, "Okay! Jimmy, I got it."

"Where y'all beautiful ladies headed?" he asked. The traffic light turned green.

"Cheddars!" I yelled.

"Why did you tell that man where we were going. We don't know him?!" Danielle exclaimed.

"It's not like he's gonna follow us," I said confidently.
Danielle kept looking out her rear-view mirror.

"Stop being scared. That man isn't following us."
As I was turning into Cheddars, Danielle turned around and said,

"I knew he was following us! That's him behind that red car!"
I parked on the back row of the parking lot trying to dodge him. When we got out of the car, Danielle saw him circling the parking lot.

"Duck" she said, pushing my head down.
We stayed low ducking behind cars until he drove out of the parking lot, and then we ran inside.

"I can't believe you told a complete stranger where we were going." Danielle declared.

"How was I supposed to know he would follow us.?" I responded.

"Whatchu mean! You can't be out here acting like a blonde!" She exclaimed.

After we finished blaming one another, we laughed and enjoyed the rest of our night.

I felt happy and secure being with Danielle, but after while I started asking myself if this is what I really wanted forever. I would ponder trying to save my marriage, but as soon as Michael would call, it would lead to an argument, and I clinged more to Danielle. I never told him that she and I were in a relationship and living together. All he knew was we were friends, and that is all I wanted him to know because there was still a part of me that knew same-sex attraction was wrong. Only certain people knew we were together. My mom and dad kept insinuating that we were together, but I would deny it.

Six months later, Michael was in town before he flew to his next duty station. I thought he might want to stay with me. I had to think of a way to sabotage that idea because Danielle was living with me. I start talking to myself to figure out my plan! Girl, you better bust a move and quickly. I started pacing the hallway, pounding my fist into the palm of my hand, I'd tell myself: *so, what I'm going to do is, tell him he can't stay with me because we aren't together anymore. You wanted a divorce—remember?!* I rehearsed my lines out loud: "Yeah that's it!" I convinced myself that would work. My phone rang and it was Michael.

"Hey, what's up?" I asked confidently.

"I'm on my way over so we can talk, and I want to see my son."

"Okay cool," I said.

I hung up and called Danielle so she wouldn't come home.

"Hey, baby can you go to your momma's house tonight, because Michael wants to come and see Lamar." I'll call you when he leaves.

Michael came over and the tension between us was obvious.

"Where's Lamar?"

"He's upstairs."

He went upstairs to spend time with our son. Later, I came up the stairs and the first thing Michael asked me was,

"Who do those clothes belong to that's in your closet?"
I had no idea he was searching my room like the FBI. He was supposed to have been in our son's room. Totally caught off guard by the question, I started fumbling over my words and looking crazy.

"Wh-What do you mean whose clothes are in my closet?"

Michael was infuriated.

"Does that gay girl live with you?!" Michael questioned.

Purposely dodging every question, I responded nonchalantly,

"What gay girl!? Stop raising your voice!"

Michael walked downstairs and slammed the door behind him. Seconds later he walked back up the stairs.

"I'm done. Sign these papers NOW!" he demanded.

I looked at the divorce papers, but I could not sign them because I wasn't certain If I truly wanted out of my marriage. Nevertheless, I had to play hard.

"I'll sign them tonight after I read over them," I said as I walked away from him.

"I'm leaving," Michael said as he went downstairs.

I walked downstairs and locked the door behind him.

The next morning Danielle came back home, and we got ready to leave for work. She and I worked together, so we rode in one vehicle. We dropped off Lamar to my mother's house and headed down the road to work. As soon as I parked, I noticed there was a car pulling up blocking me in.

"Who's that?" Danielle asked looking back.

Looking out the driver's rear-view mirror, "I have no... man, what the he--?"

It was Michael walking towards me. We kissed before we got ready to get out of the car and that's when we noticed him pulling up.

"I followed you the whole time! So, you gay now Tamika?! I knew those were her clothes in your closet. You foul!" he snapped.

"Michael, why in the hell are you following me and coming up to my job causing a scene!?"

"Damn that! Tell her to get out of the car!"

No! Leave man! *NOW*, before you get me fired!"

Michael got into his car and sped off.

Later that night I called Michael to talk. He answered the phone hesitantly and told me that he was picking up Melanie from work and he would call me back. I hung up the phone, went upstairs and gathered my things to take a shower. While I was in the shower, something made me replay the conversation Michael and I just had. Picking up Melanie from work, huh? Melanie? I was trying to place a face with a name. Wait, isn't that his ex-girlfriend? Yeah, she's the li'l shawty he was going to marry! How did I miss that? And what is he doing picking her up from work!? I jumped out of the shower still covered in soap, grabbed the towel to wipe my hands, picked up my phone and called him. "You have reached the voicemail box of 7-0-

6..." This nigga has my calls going straight to voicemail, but he wants to play the victim about Danielle. I sent him a text that said, *"Please, please make sure you and ya' girl pick up these divorce papers tomorrow."* After I sent the text, I was in my feelings, so I went to play Apple Music and, turned on *Love Is Blind* by Eve. I slid my phone on the counter and got back in the shower. As the song played, *"Love is Blind, and it'll take over your mind. Whatcha think is love, it's truly not..."*

"SHO'LL AIN'T!" I blurted out.

I woke up the following morning to a voicemail from Michael and three missed calls. Later, that day, I heard a knock at the door. Looking through the blinds, I saw him standing there and I opened the door.

"Did you have a good time with your boo? Your phone dies quick in her presence. She drained the life out of you and your phone huh?"

"Whatever Tamika," he snapped.

"Yeah, I bet it is whatever. So, did you have sex with her?"

He just stood there.

"Hello! You went deaf?!"

"Yes, I slept with her," he answered.

"Wowwww! At least you're bold about it. I'll pass on a conversation. Your son is upstairs and after you see him you can dismiss yourself." I said walking into the kitchen.

Michael walked upstairs and after a couple hours he came back downstairs.

"I love you. Let's talk," He declared.

Walking towards the door, I responded, "Nah, I'm straight. Goodbye."

Locking the door behind him, so many emotions hit me at once, I could not think straight. I went up to my room and just laid in bed until I fell asleep.

A couple of weeks later Michael called and said that he arranged for the movers to come pack up my home, and he already purchased plane tickets for Lamar and me to fly to Washington.

"The movers will be there tomorrow at Noon. If you don't

> I don't know if I can be with a woman forever. *If only she was a man.* I thought.

want to come, let me know and I'll cancel the appointment."

I was not expecting to hear any of this.

"I'll call you back and let you know." I replied.

Faced with a major decision in less than 24 hours about what I want to do with my life left me stuck between a rock and a hard place. Things were not great with Michael and me. We did not get along, but he wanted us to catch a flight which means leaving Danielle. I genuinely care about her. She is really in love with me and I promised to never break her heart. It would be devastating to my mind to know that I hurt her. She is the only person that genuinely has my back, but I don't know If I can be with a woman forever. *If only she was a man.* I thought. My head started to hurt trying to figure out a decision. What am I going to do? Catch a flight for Michael or stay with Danielle?

Three: Conflicted

Emotions

"Welcome to Seattle Tacoma International Airport," said the flight attendant over the intercom. "Please remain seated until the plane is parked at the gate."

Lamar and I were eager to get off the plane to view the city. Once we got cleared to exit the plane, we grabbed our things and rushed over to baggage claim.

"Where's daddy?" Lamar asked as we stood there waiting on our luggage.

"He was supposed to meet us here. I'm about to call him right now."

As I held the phone to my ear, suddenly all I heard around me were soft whispers and voices saying, "Aww, awww, that's so sweet!" Hundreds of people were standing around with their luggage staring directly at me. With a puzzled look on my face, I turned around to see why I was the center of attention. Michael was behind me on one knee holding a ring.

"Mrs. Ingram, will you marry me again?" he proposed.

In total shock, I froze holding my hands over my mouth. Unable to get a word out, a lady yelled in excitement,

"SAY YES GIRL!"

I removed my hands from over my mouth. Blushing and smiling from ear to ear,

"Yes!" I happily replied.

He placed the ring on my finger, and we shared a kiss.

After viewing the city and riding on the Ferry to Oak Harbor, we finally made it to our new home. Oak Harbor Washington was quiet and peaceful. The sun shines so bright you can see the sun rays beaming through the clouds illuminating the city. Everyone minds their own business, and the crime rate is slim to none. You could leave your door unlocked and still feel safe. It was the perfect place to start a family.

Michael and I decided to start over with a clean slate. Our lives started to feel like a fairytale. We went out on dates, cuddled on the sofa to watch movies every night, I cooked his favorite dishes and served him. I was so ecstatic, I even learned how to play his favorite video game, *Call of Duty*. To my surprise, I enjoyed playing it. Family nights were the best because we would always go buy a bunch of snacks, play games, and watch movies with our son.

Several months later, on a Wednesday morning, the birds were chirping, and the sun lit up the room waking me up. I woke up smiling and feeling joyous. I began to clean up, wash clothes, and make Michael's lunch. He always came home for lunch. After I finished preparing lunch, I sat down on the couch and popped in *Mortal Kombat*. Michael always beat me at that game, and I wanted to teach myself how to play. I could not wait for him to come home so I could kick his butt. When he came home, he embraced me, and we kissed.

"How's work so far baby?" I asked as I was bringing his lunch to him.

"I'm ready to be off baby," he said.

"Soooo, do you want to play Mortal Kombat!?"

Michael shook his head. "Baby you're gonna lose."

"I know, but maybe you can teach me," I replied.

As soon as we started playing, I started doing all the tricks and combos. The perplexed look on his face was hilarious. *"FINISH HIM"* the narrator said in the game. I did a specialty move.

"You've been learning how to play this whole time just so you could win!" Michael shouted laughingly. I burst out laughing. "Gotcha!"

It was almost time for Michael to go back

> "Never mind, you're kissing me like a woman."

to work. Before he left, we kissed as usual. He pulled me closer.

"I want a better kiss," he insisted.

We began to share a deeper kiss, but he pulled away and said,

"Never mind. You're kissing me like a woman." And then he left. I was standing there thinking, Wow! Did he just say that to me? *That remark really hurt my feelings.* I texted him, *"Why would you say that to me? I wasn't thinking of another woman when we kissed and that's the same way I've been kissing you."*

He texted back, *"You still got a thing for women because that's how women kiss each other."* His words felt like he took a sharp knife and pierced it through my heart causing my self-esteem to bleed out slowly. When he came home from work, he apologized and asked for forgiveness. I forgave him and put on a facade that I was okay, but the thought never left my mind.

Every day that passed by, I felt empty, hurt, and rejected inside. I could not get the image of how he looked at me as if I disgusted him out of my head. Michael was not showing that passion he once had for me. He told me that we had sex occasionally, like old people. I really wanted to be into him, but my body was not reacting. Our intimacy started to run dry, because I no longer knew how to express my love to him. My experience with men had always been devastating. My confidence faded, and I started to think that maybe I was better off with a woman, and I should have never broken up with Danielle. Then I started feeling guilty because we were together in the first place. The flame for my marriage was beginning to burn out like a candle running out of wick. We had some good days but the bad was starting to outweigh the good.

One evening, I was upstairs having a full concert with myself. My Favorite songs were playing. I started singing out loud and dancing while putting away some folded clothes. The concert quickly turned into the hood version when *Knock Knock* by Monica came on. I grabbed my husband's doo-rag and tied it around my head, grabbed my comb to represent the microphone and put on my shades off the dresser. I started slapping and kicking the air while rolling my neck in the mirror rapping, *"Make me wanna ride pass ya house and sit. Kick down ya doors and smack ya chick! Just to show you Monica not havin' dat! So, in love with witchu like…"*

"Tamika!" Michael shouted.

I immediately jumped in fright as Michael shouted over the music.

"I didn't hear you coming. You scared me. What's up with you? You only call me by my name when you're mad?"

"Nothing baby, I was trying to get your attention." Michael handed me the phone. "It's Shanelle." Shanelle is my younger sister. She is very funny, bold and outspoken.

"Yo! Talk to me, just don't lie to me baby."

She laughed. "Mika why are you so lame bruh?! Listen, I called to tell you about what I just found out."

"Ok, lemme sit down girl, so I can hear this." As my sister began filling me in on the details, I heard somebody from downstairs pick up the phone.

"Shhhh, be quiet." I whispered. "Did you hear that?"

"Yeah somebody picked up the phone." Seconds later I heard the phone click off.

"Ok, go ahead." We continued out our conversation and got off the phone.

Michael walks in the room. "What was that all about?" he said irritated while walking up on me.

"Nothing. She told me something that went down at my daddy's house."

Michael looked at me in rage. "So why did you get quiet when you heard me pick up the other end and try to rush off the phone when you

> My life flashed before my eyes; I began to fade out trying to gasp for air!

heard me coming? And who else was on the phone?" I was confused as I stared back at him.

"Man, what are you talking about? And back up off me."

Michael got in my face and we started arguing. He wrapped his hands around my neck and started choking me while fussing. Looking up at him, I could not hear the words he was saying, because my vision was beginning to blur as his grip around my neck got tighter and tighter. My life flashed before my eyes; I began to fade out trying to gasp for air! As I fought to remove his hands from around my neck, all I remember is praying to God that Michael would let me go, and suddenly he did and walked away. Immediately I burst into tears. I was angry and afraid. I put on my shoes, grabbed my son, and walked out the house to my neighbor's house and called the police.

When the military police arrived, they took Michael away, and he had to stay in the barracks for a week. He could have crushed my windpipe and killed me. My life seemed like a living hell and the only positive thing was my son. All I had was me. I could not call my parents and tell them what I was going through because I did not want them in my business. For the remainder of the night, all I did was cry. The type of cry that makes you pause, and it feels like your heart stops beating for a couple seconds. My emotions started fluctuating up and down like a roller coaster. One minute I was crying because I was sad.

The next minute I was crying because I wanted to go home. I was crying because I was afraid. Then, I was crying because I was mad.

The next morning, I woke up angry. The spirit of vengeance began to rise on the inside of me. Rocking back and forth on the living room sofa, all sorts of thoughts came to mind to make Michael hurt the way he made me hurt. I thought about burning all his clothes, pouring bleach in the game system, throwing away all his sneakers or cutting up his uniforms.

"That's it!" I said mischievously.

Michael kept all his uniforms in the downstairs closet. I grabbed one, went to the kitchen, grabbed the scissors, and came back to the living room. I started cutting the uniform and realized he can just buy another one. Hanging the uniform back in the closet already cut up, I started to think of another plan. He needed to have a near death experience the same way I did.

The week ended and Michael came home showing empathy and being apologetic while I was in the kitchen putting away the dishes.

"Baby, I'll never put my hands on you again," he said pitifully.

Giving Michael the cold shoulder, I snatched away from his embrace.

"Baby, I'm so sorry. My intentions were not to put my hands on you. I was upset because I thought you were trying to be sneaky."

He kept trying to console me and the feel of his touch made me pop like a shaken soda bottle.

"MICHAEL, SHUT THE HELL UP TALKING TO ME! I DON'T WANNA HEAR SHIT YOU GOTTA SAY!" I was so furious; I shattered a glass plate on the floor. "YOU COULD'VE KILLED ME! LEAVE ME ALONE, SERIOUSLY!"

He walked away sensing there was nothing he could do to placate me. That incident changed the trajectory of our marriage. I did not view him the same as before. I reverted to my old, cold ways.

Week after week I continued my normal daily routine of cooking, cleaning, and spending time with Lamar. During his nap time, I called Danielle. That was typically around the time I called every day. We had been talking every day since Michael was in the barracks. I told her how sorry I was for breaking up with her and how much I missed her. She did not forgive me instantly, but she told me we could try to rebuild a friendship. Danielle had no idea about where I was or what was really going on. I wanted her to think I was doing good in ATL at my aunt's house. If Danielle knew what was going on, she would have been livid. I ended up getting caught talking to her, and she found out. Michael was really upset when he found out she and I had started back talking, but I did not care at all because I was just counting down the days until I would leave.

It was around Thanksgiving time, and I wanted to go home.

"Please don't leave me alone for the holidays?" Michael pleaded.

"It's just thanksgiving. We will spend Christmas together," I said reluctantly.

I booked the flight. The following week Lamar and I were on the plane headed back to Columbus. We landed and waited on my parents to pick us up from the airport. When they pulled up, Lamar and I were so happy to see them! We ran and hugged them tight before we got in the car. I was so glad to just be free and happy.

Thanksgiving Day Danielle texted me, "*I made it.*" She had flown in from basic training. After I spent time with my family, I went to her hotel room to see her. Danielle told me how bad I hurt her by leaving her for Michael. Watching her cry was so hard for me to see. Guilt hovered over me so strong, I could feel the weight of it. Grabbing her hands and looking into her eyes I said,

"I'm truly sorry," I said regretfully.

She forgave me, and I gave her a hug. We started to talk and laugh again after that. The whole time we were together, I started having mixed emotions again about my identity and my sexuality because with her I was simply happy versus being with a man. The more thought I gave it, the more confused I got, so I stopped caring and did what made me happy. Danielle and I spent the rest of the day together because she had to be back in Texas the next day.

It was the morning after Thanksgiving. Danielle and

> I stopped caring and did what made me happy.

I woke up early to go out for breakfast together before she left for Texas. I was headed back to my dad's house after breakfast when my phone rang. It was Michael calling.

"Good Morning," I answered in a low-spirited tone.

"What time will you guys be flying in so I can be at the airport? I miss y'all," he replied.

"I don't know. I'm driving right now," I said hesitantly.

"Okay, can you call me back and let me know?" he asked.

I paused for about 15 seconds before responding,

"We're not coming back."

Four: Plot Twist

Coming home for Thanksgiving was my way out. The plan was to never go back. Michael called me right back after I hung up.

"What do you mean y'all aren't coming back?" he questioned.

"I don't want to be with you anymore," I said, and I hung up.

Seconds later, my phone rings,

"Helloooooooo . . ." I answered singing melodiously.

"Tamika don't do this, please!" Michael begged.

"Look Michael, I don't want you anymore."

"Are you leaving me for Danielle?"

"Nope. Now goodbye," I replied.

Every time Michael called, the more resentful I became.

"LEAVE ME ALONE. I'M ABOUT TO BLOCK YOU!" I threatened. That did not stop him, he continued to call back to back for hours. I ignored all the calls.

Later, I went to my mom's house. She asked me when Lamar and I were leaving, but before I could answer, her phone started ringing.

"Hold on. This is your husband."

I thought he was about to tell her everything. I was trying to ear hustle, but it was unsuccessful, so I tried to make sense of the conversation based on my mother's responses. My mother got up and walked in her room. That ruined my plan. Shanelle came into the living room and we started to converse.

"When are you and my nephew leaving?" she asked.

SIGH. "We're not."

Shanelle stood up, "What happened?"

I started telling her what happened, and she got upset.

"What! Did that nigga touch my nephew?!" she shouted.

I shook my head no.

"Don't tell me nothing else right now!" she stormed off.

When my mother got off the phone, she came into the living room.

"Michael is so hurt. He's crying so hard begging me to talk you into getting on the plane. What in the world are you doing?" she asked.

I thought to myself—Mission Accomplished!

"I don't want to be with him anymore." I said cautiously since I was trying to keep her out of my personal life.

"I hope you're not leaving over that *Danielle girl!*" my mother emphasized.

My mother was totally against lesbianism, and she hated the thought of Danielle and me. I felt it was a lost cause talking to her about how I truly felt because she was *team Michael* no matter what. Even if I were leaving him for her, my mother would never understand. In her eyes he was gold. "No ma'am I just don't want to be with him anymore." replying with an attitude.

> My mother was totally against lesbianism . . . she was *team Michael* no matter what.

"Well I hope you know what you're doing Tamika."

When my mother closed her room door, I picked my phone up and saw 11 missed calls from Michael. Still hurting inside, I ignored and started watching TV.

Moving back home forced me to start over and get back on my feet. Every morning I woke up putting in job applications. Also, I went down to the Department of Labor to apply for food stamps. Living with my dad and his wife became stressful because they kept hounding me about being over my mother's house.

"Why are you living here if you're going to be at your momma's house every day?" My dad asked with an attitude.

"Since you're over there all day just live with yo' momma." Jessica chimed in.

They go to work all day so what difference does it make where I go and who I decide to spend my time with? The vibes around the house were shady and I didn't want to be disrespectful with my response, so I didn't respond. I called my mom and asked to live with her.

Every day I called my dad to ask him if my food stamp card had arrived in the mail.

"No, it hasn't come yet. I'll let you know," he said.

"Okay, please don't forget, because I really need to buy food for Lamar and me."

Days went by and I had not heard anything. I called my dad again,

"Did my food stamp card come yet?" I asked.

I could hear Jessica in the background being loud and irate saying,

"Tell her don't be sending shit over here. She doesn't live here!"

My daddy responded, "Yes, it came, but you don't live here so your mail shouldn't come here anymore."

Ignoring Jessica in the background I said, "Okay, I'm about to come get my card."

Jessica continued yelling in the background, "Tell her she can't come get shit over here!"

I could feel my temperature rising as the provoking continued.

"Lord please help me," I mumbled under my breath. "Daddy, I'm on my way to get my card, because I really need it."

"Naw, don't come. We threw the card in the trash because you don't live here." he replied.

My dad flipped the script and jumped on board with Jessica's evilness. I erupted like a volcano at 1,200 degrees Celsius.

"WHAT KIND OF DAD ARE YOU!? WHO DOES THIS!? I'M ON MY WAY TO BEAT YO' WIFE'S ASS! WHEN I PULL UP, TELL HER TO BRING HER ASS OUTSIDE! I DONT GIVE A DAMN ANYMORE, BECAUSE I'VE HAD ENOUGH! PUT ME ON SPEAKER PHONE, I'LL TELL HER MYSELF!" I screamed.

My dad threatened to call the police if I came over.

"I SWEAR ON MY LIFE, YOU'LL NEVER HEAR FROM ME OR LAMAR EVER AGAIN!" I threatened.

I hung up the phone on him. Hearing all the noise in the living room, my mom came in and asked what was going on. After she heard the story, she talked and prayed with me so I could calm down. The anger I had towards them turned to pure hatred.

A couple weeks passed without hearing a word from Michael. On a Monday morning Michael called waking me from my sleep.

"Hello?" I whispered.

"I have started the divorce process. I've scheduled and paid for a DNA test with LabCorp." he said.

Sitting up from the couch and snatching the covers back, I asked him, "Man, what the hell? Are you really calling me with this?!" I was totally flabbergasted.

"Yeah, I don't believe Lamar is mine, and I've been carrying the thought for years," he responded.

I hung up the phone in his face.

Sitting on the edge of the couch, I could feel the anxiety resting on my shoulders and my right leg began to shake.

"MA! MA!" I yelled. "Come here!"

My mom came walking into the living room from her bedroom. "You better want something–yelling my name like that. Now what is it?" she asked.

"Michael called me saying that he wants a DNA test and he already paid for it. He said I need to take Lamar to LabCorp."

"A DNA test! You think he's doing this because you left him?" she asked.

"Seems that way. Suddenly, he wants a DNA test. He never asked for one before." I replied.

"Well, you did hurt the man, and now he's lashing out. Calm down and just go take the test and get it over with. You do know he's the father, right?" she asked.

Taking a deep breath with my hands over my face, I replied, "Yeah, I'm positive."

Later that day, Lamar and I went down to LabCorp for the testing. When we walked into the building, it was cold. There were lots of people in the waiting room, I thought, *I'm going to be in here forever.* I walked up to the front desk, signed in, and sat down. Lamar and I played a game on my phone while waiting to be called.

"Tamika Ingram," called the nurse technician while standing at the door holding a clipboard. She was quite pleasant and professional.

"Hello, my name is Ruby. Follow me, please," she directed me. We followed her to the room, and she asked me to verify my son's information. Watching her swab my son's mouth was so embarrassing. I could not believe this was really happening.

"All set," she said. "We will email you the results within four to five business days. Good luck!" Ruby walked us out of the room showing us how to exit out of the building.

Walking to my car I thought to myself, "Four to five business days seems like a long time when you are waiting on confirmation or results from something." I knew that if I kept thinking about it, it would just drag the days out. While I was strapping Lamar in his car seat, my phone started ringing. After I finished strapping Lamar in, I grabbed my phone, but I missed the call. It was Michael. He left a voicemail *"You need to let me know if you want this furniture or not because...."* I took the phone away from my face and ended the voicemail. Listening to it and his voice upset me and, I knew it was not a good idea to listen to the rest. Lamar and I went out to eat, to the mall, and out for ice cream to take my mind off everything. That worked for the moment, but while I was going through constant hell, it was hard to take my mind off things completely.

Saturday morning, I was sitting on my bed scrolling through my email to track some shoes I ordered online. As I scrolled through my inbox, I saw an email from Lab Corp that said *Test Results*. I opened the email immediately and started reading the email. I opened the attached file but overlooked the testing charts with columns and random numbers because they were

> I saw an email from Lab Corp that said, *Test Results.*

confusing. Instead, I read the paragraph under the chart that said:

> *The alleged father, <u>Michael Ingram</u> is* **Excluded** *as the biological father of <u>Lamar Ingram.</u> The conclusion is based on the non-matching alleles observed at the loci listed above with a PI equal to 0. The alleged father lacks the genetic markers that must be contributed to the child by the biological father.* **The probability of paternity is 0%.***"*

I was completely astonished, and my heart dropped immediately. I could feel it beating out of my chest, I felt knots in my throat, and it felt like my vocal cords collapsed because I was unable to speak. All I could do was think about how everybody was going to talk about me, ridicule me, and view me differently. Most importantly, I had to face Michael, and that thought alone made me nauseated. I was crushed, ashamed and humiliated. I felt like I was on a talk show like the Maury Show. I could imagine Maury saying,

"When it comes down to three-year-old Lamar.... Michael, you are NOT the father!"

I would be the devastated woman that runs off the stage crying and falling out on the floor! This was the biggest blow I had ever faced. After reading the paragraph over and over, I started hating myself, because I honestly believed Michael was the father.

It took me a week to accept the paternity results. The whole week I did not eat, sleep, or talk to anyone. I stayed locked up in my room mostly. Michael called me, but I was not ready to face him, so I ignored the call. Guilt and depression came in, and the thought of suicide began to bombard my thoughts. Every day I would try to face my reality, but I was not strong enough. One day my little sister Shanelle asked me to take her to her friend's house for a get together. I took her. When we got there, I walked inside to speak and decided to stay awhile to clear my mind. Everybody was drinking and passing blunts. Every time the blunt came to me, I passed. When it came back around my sister said in a forceful tone,

"Hit the blunt, Mika! You look like you need to hit it."

"I don't know how to smoke," I said.

She put the blunt in my hand and said, "Now inhale it. Hold it in. Now exhale."

As the smoke started coming out of my mouth, she smiled saying, "Yeahhhhhh, that's how you do it! Now hit it again!"

I hit every blunt that came around. That night I was so high, whatever problem I did have seemed to disappear.

I decided to face my biggest fear when I woke up the next day. While the phone was ringing, I could feel my nerves rising. I closed my eyes and took a deep breath exhaling slowly. *"You have reached the voicemail box..."* Michael did not answer. When I hung up the phone, a text message flashed across that said, **"Don't ever call or speak to me again. I have nothing to say to you."** I called right back after reading the message, but he ignored me again. *"Please answer the phone. I am so sorry. I really didn't know."* I texted. Michael never responded. I waited a couple hours and tried to call back, but he sent me to voicemail again.

I started thinking about the DNA test results while lying in bed. All signs pointed to Dwayne. "Ah hell naw," I murmured, throwing my hands up in the air. The only way I knew to find him was through Facebook™. After I typed in his name, I began to scroll until I saw his profile picture. When I found him, I pulled up his page and looked through his photos. "Oh...My...God!" I said staring at a picture of his daughter. Dwayne's daughter looks just like Lamar's baby pictures. The more I kept staring, reality began to set in. I sent Dwayne a message: *"Hey, I know it's been three years since we've spoken but it's very urgent that we talk. There's something I have to tell you. When would be a good time to talk?"*

Four days passed and Dwayne never responded. I went back to his Facebook page, clicked on his wife's page, and sent her a message. *"Hey Angela, how are you? My name is Tamika. I'm not writing to you to start any drama. I am trying to reach your husband to let him know that we have a son together and reaching out to you is my last option. If you could please tell him to check his messages or you can call me at 706-555-----."* Within minutes she responded back to me. While we were on the phone, I began to fill her in on the past relationship I had with Dwayne. We discovered that my son is older than their son by one month. She said that she would like for all of us

to meet at Denny's.

"Can you bring your son too?" Angela asked.

"I sure will," I said. We agreed to meet later that evening.

Lamar and I arrived at Denny's and waited in the lobby area until

Angela and Dwayne walked in. When I saw Dwayne opening the door,

I looked at him in disgust.

"Hi, I'm Angela. Nice to meet you," she said introducing herself.

"I'm Tamika and this is my son Lamar," I responded politely.

"Hey Lamar! He looks just like our son D.J." she said. Dwayne

stood there silent looking clueless as if he had never seen me before in

life. Everything in me wanted his face to greet the palm of my hand,

but I kept my cool. They sat down, and we decided to schedule a DNA

test to confirm paternity.

Sitting in the lobby at LabCorp for the second time was beyond

embarrassing. "Lord please don't let anyone recognize me, I mumbled

under my breath."

"Tamika Ingram and Dwayne Brown," called a nurse technician

from the doorway. When we got to the back, Dwayne and I never said

a word to one another. The moment was awkward, and I tried my best to not look in his direction. We went through the process at the Lab and left. Four days later the results came back and stated,

> The alleged father <u>Dwayne Brown</u> **cannot be excluded** as the biological father of <u>Lamar Ingram</u>. Based on testing results obtained from analyses of the DNA loci listed, **the probability of paternity is 99.9998%.**

All I could think about was Michael. I called him, but he sent me to voicemail. Flying back to Washington and begging for his forgiveness was the only option I had left to make this right. I texted him, *"Michael I know you are ignoring me, and I don't blame you. I just want you to know that I am booking a flight to come back to Washington in hopes that you will talk to me."* He immediately responded. *"Don't waste your time. There is nothing you can say or do Tamika. I'm done."*

"Damn!" I shouted. "I've messed up big time"

Five: Enough Is Enough

Flying back to Washington was not a wise decision, but the guilt of Michael not being the father was too much to bear. Even though I knew Dwayne was Lamar's biological father, when I got to Washington, Michael gave me an ultimatum to be with him. He said that he didn't want Dwayne to have anything to do with Lamar if I were going to stay. I decided to stay with Michael eventhough he still reminded me that I was wrong, and sometimes threatened to tell Lamar the truth. I apologized to Michael every day and, I catered to him even when he rejected it. He made me suffer because he was hurting. Life was miserable for me. As the pressure of life intensified, my mind felt trapped inside of a bag slowly losing oxygen. I did not know who I was or if I was coming or going most days. On the days Michael would come home, I went to the gym for an hour. Working out was the only thing keeping my sanity until I started going to church. Eventually Michael started going with me and we started attending Marriage Counseling. Things seemingly appeared to shift between us for the good and we stayed in Washington for several months before coming back to Columbus.

When we got back to Columbus, I got a job at Hollister. Working at a clothing store, I never realized how much slavery work goes into keeping the store neat and organized. Customers would come into the store slinging shirts and pulling pants from the bottom of the stack causing all the folded pants to fall over. They would stand there, and watch clothes hit the floor and walk off. I spent most of my shift fuming, calming myself down and refolding clothes. A lady came into the store getting ready to yank a size X-Large shirt from the bottom of the stack. I ran over to her saying,

"Ma'am don't pull that shirt. Pick up the stack of shirts that are sitting on top first." I hated that job.

I got off work one night and decided to unwind and watch a movie with Michael. We were in the living room. He was lying on the love seat and I was lying on the sofa. I called his name, but he did not hear me, so I picked up a pillow and tossed it on the couch he was lying on.

"Babe!" I yelled.

He got mad and started cursing me out because I threw the pillow.

"Let's go in the room and talk," I insisted.

I did not want to fuss around Lamar. When we got in the room, Michael went left. The pillow toss somehow triggered a past emotion. He started talking about his childhood saying he is about to torture me the way he was tortured. I looked at him like he was out of his mind.

"Torture me? You sound *ridiculous*. I'm about to go," I said.

> I knew I had to fight my way out or die trying.

As I walked towards the door, Michael pulled me back and pushed me on the floor. He picked up some DVDs and started tossing them at me like frisbees while walking closer to me. Dodging DVDs, I tried to escape the room, but he picked me up saying,

"Yo' ass about to see how it feels to suffer!" he shouted as he slammed me on the bed.

I swiftly jumped up and Michael head butted me causing me to fall backwards on the bed. He grabbed a suitcase, started beating me with it, then put the suitcase on top of me and sat on it crushing my body. I knew I had to fight my way out or die trying. The weight of the suitcase and his body on top of me felt like life was being squeezed out of me. I laid there in excruciating pain suffering silently, because if I would have started yelling my son would have heard me. Michael sat on me for about 5 minutes talking recklessly, calling me out of my name. When he got off me, I turned into a psychopathic maniac throwing heels, picture frames and whatever else I could hit him with yelling,

"You wanna fight? Nigga let's fight! I'm tired of you puttin' yo damn hands on me! I can show you a looney tune! I'm not a weak ass woman you think you're just gonna beat on!"

I ran over to him, started punching, slapping, and kicking him. When I started to fight back, Michael stopped hitting me. I went to the bathroom, slammed the door. While staring in the mirror at myself, I saw there were bruises, cuts on my arm, scars, and blood dripping down my face. One of my fingernails was gone to the white meat. I needed to get away. Leaving the house in shorts, a shirt, and some flip flops, I walked for miles in pitch black darkness. There were no streetlights on. It was very cold and windy outside, but my mind was so far gone, I could not feel a thing. My mind and my thoughts were submerged in darkness. The further I walked down the street; my stride started slowing down. I could feel my body aching and my head started spinning.

"AHHHHHHHHHH!" I screamed before falling to the ground. I released the loudest scream I could from deep within my soul. I sat on the side of the curb rocking back and forth. After a few minutes of trying to get myself together, I walked all the way to his auntie's house and stayed there for a couple days.

After a couple days passed, I decided to visit my mom's house.

"Come here," she said, squinting trying to see my face from afar. "How did you get that scar on your face?"

At that moment, I could feel myself cracking and tears started to fill my eyes. Playing it cool and blinking away the tears, I looked away.

"I don't know "I believe I scratched myself by mistake." I really wanted to unravel like tissue into my mother's arms, vent, and release everything I had been carrying inside. Life was taking a toll on my brain and my body. There was so much build up, I did everything I could each day to push into another day.

I finally got a call from TSYS for an interview. God finally blessed me with a better job. There I met a woman named Tiffany in orientation. She was hilarious, sweet, and we clicked instantly. Her vibes were always positive and anytime I was down, she was there to snap me out of it. There were plenty of times I stayed with her just to avoid going home. When I graduated from orientation, I was placed in the call center. Totally lost and confused, I called Escalations on every call. Escalations was the help line. This woman by the name of Tiana Ingram always had a nice tone and willingness to help me. We shared the same last name and that caught my attention. I sent her an instant message that said, *"Hey, I'm new on the floor and I want you to know you're the coolest! Thank you for all your help. Your other team members are rude."*

She responded *"Thanks, anytime!"* and we conversed on messenger every day after for weeks.

Tiana and I became messenger friends. I felt like we were on a chat line because I had never seen her before. I sent her a message. *"Can I see you? We talk every day and we've never seen one another."*

"Yes," she responded. *"I'll come over when I finish this call."*

As I was on a call, I looked up to see this beautiful woman with the skin color of a smooth Chocolate Mocha, brown eyes, and long curly hair secretly tiptoeing around the corner. I glanced up and saw her snow-white teeth and high cheekbones creating the most gorgeous smile I've ever seen.

"Thank you for calling TD Card Services and have a wonderful day," I expressed to the customer. While I was wrapping up the call, Tiana began looking at the pictures on my desk.

"You have a nice family. What's your son's name?"

"Thank you. His name is Lamar. Why were you tiptoeing over here?" I asked amused.

"Oh wow! I have always wanted a son named Lamar. Man, you never know who's watching you."

We laughed and talked until my fifteen-minute break was over. Tiana wrote her number on my whiteboard.

"Call me tonight," she said smiling and walking away.

I pondered on whether I should call her.

Three days later I decided to text Tiana while I was at work. *"Hey this is Tamika. I get off work at 11, can I call you then?"*

"Yes," she texted back.

When I got out, I called her, and we talked my whole way home.

"When are we going to hang out?" I asked.

"We can hang out any time after 5 o'clock," Tiana replied.

"Okay, cool! I'll text you in the morning. Goodnight."

I loved her personality! We had a lot of things in common like gospel music, food, hobbies, and church. Talking to her was a breath of fresh air and I knew we would be cool.

Michael wanted to start back going to marriage counseling as a last attempt to salvage our marriage. I was against marriage counseling. It was hard enough to grasp the sermons at church between the gossip, drama, jealousy, and favoritism going on. I would go to church half full and come out empty. There were days I went to church dumb and came out dumber. To attend marriage counseling would surely end the 0.36% of marriage we had left but I participated anyway. Every week I had to have one-on-one sessions with Co-Pastor Stacy. The sessions turned into me being the counselor, and I was encouraging her every week. After several sessions, I decided to drop out.

One afternoon when I got off work early, I went to pick up Lamar from the after-school program, took him to McDonald's and then we went home. As I was helping him with homework, I received a text

from Tiana that said, *"Hey what's up?"*

"Nothing, helping Lamar with his homework." I texted back.

Thirty minutes later Tiana replied, *"I'm finna chill, have a li'l*

smoke session and burn a couple Ls. You can come over if you want."

Staring at my phone reading, "burn a couple Ls", I assumed she meant

smoking weed. *Send me your address,* I replied. When Michael came

home, I put my shoes on and sent a text to Tiana, *"on my way."*

After putting the address in the GPS my phone rings.

"Yeah," I answered annoyed.

"Where are you going?" Michael asked

"To my friend's house. I'll be back," I responded.

"I'm outside." I texted Tiana. She came downstairs to meet me and

together we walked to her apartment. Walking through her living

room to the balcony, I saw candles lit on the breakfast bar. "What

candle fragrance is that? I asked. It smells really good."

"Thank You. Mahogany Teakwood from Bath and Body Works."

Standing outside on the balcony she offered me a seat, lit a blunt

and passed it to me. Tiana and I were so high our eyes were low and red. I began to confide in her about being sexually out of tune with my body.

"I think my body is broken and that bothers me a lot."

Tiana gave me a confused look.

"What do you mean by that?" she asked me.

"It's like I'm never sexually stimulated whenever I have sex, and I don't enjoy it," I explained.

> Recognizing that I was sexually aroused by her blew my mind. ...

We sat outside for hours talking. She cracked a joke and we started to laugh. Laughing turned into kissing and kissing turned into intimacy. Recognizing that I was sexually aroused by her blew my mind and I didn't know what to think.

"I have to go," I said, rushing to get to my car.

Riding home, I went into deep thought. *What's REALLY going on?* I have experienced a female before, but it was nothing like this. My first girlfriend was more of a reassuring place for me. The way I felt with Tiana was on a different level. My body automatically synced with hers and my body had never synced with anyone before. I enjoyed sexual intimacy for the very first time. She took her time with me and cared for my wants and needs. Every guy just did what they had to do to climax. It was not just about the sex, she believed in my dreams, she pushed me, encouraged me, and complimented me on my worst looking day. I connected with her physically mentally and emotionally.

My marriage had run its course. My presence was there physically, but mentally and emotionally I was absent. There was no fight left in me. One morning after dropping Lamar off at school, Michael called, and we got into a heated argument. He said that he married me for all the wrong reasons and regretted ever marrying me.

"The feeling is mutual sir." I responded.

Michael was pissed off. "I'm throwing all of your clothes outside in the yard!" he yelled.

He could have burned them all for all I cared at that point. That was my last argument. I was so sick of the circular motion and the going back and forth. I was done.

When Michael left for class, I went back to the house and grabbed all of Lamar's clothes, majority of my things and called Tiffany to take me over to my sister's house. When I got to my sister's house, I told her that I needed to stay with her for a while until I figured out my next move. My sister came into the living room combing her hair,

"Mika! You should have been left. Listen, hold on," she said turning down the music. "If you go back to him don't ever talk to me again and that's on God. 'Nye don't eat all my snacks because they gotta last."

Shanelle walked back to her bathroom and turned the music back up. I called Tiana and told her everything that happened. She clocked out, brought me her car, and told me to move all my things to her place.

"Take me back to work and handle your business. Pick me up at 5 o'clock. Here is the house key. You and Lamar can stay with me until you find a place to stay," she insisted.

I went and grabbed the rest of my things, leaving the keys, my wedding ring and everything else behind.

Six: Trapped

I moved in with Tiana and never looked back. She watched Lamar every night I went to work. Lamar loved to learn and so did Tiana. They were two peas in a pod watching *Jeopardy* every evening and bonding stronger each day. I met Tiana's daughter Nicole. She was just like me, extremely dramatic and silly. We hung out all the time, taking pictures, making videos, and getting our nails done. We became inseparable, and I loved her like she was my daughter. The bond Lamar and Nicole had was instant. You would think they grew up together from birth. They told everybody they were brother and sister. Tiana and Lamar did everything together from playing to sleeping. Family days were F-U-N fun and exciting! We all dressed alike and played games, made music videos, and some nights we would create our own cooking show. Everyone was locked in and over time we became a blended family without force.

Michael was a distant memory until one day while I was at the mall shopping for Lamar's Kindergarten graduation, he called saying he wanted his family back. I declined the offer and blocked him faster than the blink of an eye. I started researching divorce procedures. Being free from him was refreshing as a dip in the pool. The weight of stress, bondage and being unhappy was over. I was so happy; I spoke to everybody that passed me in the mall.

The day had come for Tiana to meet my father. I needed someone to pick Lamar up from school. He was my last resort and it took everything in me to call him. I was not able to pick Lamar up from my dad's house because I worked late, so I asked Tiana to pick him up for me. Sounding uncertain she asked,

"Are you sure you're ready for me to meet your dad?"

"*SIGH,* I don't have a choice but to be ready. I told him you were on the way. Let me know how it goes." Before Tiana could call me back, my dad called.

"Tiana just left from picking up Lamar. She seems cool but let me address that I noticed the

> "I pray to God you're not gay."

way she dresses. She had on a button-down shirt and a pair of dress shoes that I have in my closet." My daddy was being dramatic, and I was not in the mood to entertain him.

"Okay daddy, thanks. I'll talk to you later. I have to go."

I could sense the agitation in his voice,

"You trying to blow me off, but I pray to God you're not gay."

"Bye daddy" I said and hung up.

Tiana called shortly after and told me that she needed to come and get something out of my car. She came inside, got the keys from me, and left. Realizing she had been gone for quite some time I called, but she did not answer. About thirty minutes later, Tiana comes back to my desk livid.

"What's wrong babe?" I asked.

"I found your secret phone you had hidden in your car! You're a liar, and I no longer want to be with you!"

My whole face froze stiff like ice.

"This job is the only thing that's saving your life right now." She walked away from me. The second phone I had was to talk to Danielle. I really did not want Danielle to know that I was in a relationship with another woman because being with a woman was the sole reason she and I broke up. My brain was fried, I had to soak in the fact that I was busted being sneaky. Knowing Tiana was hurt, I clocked out early to fix everything by calling Danielle and being honest about everything. Danielle was furious!

"REALLY! YOU SAID YOU'D NEVER BE WITH ANOTHER WOMAN, AND HERE YOU ARE IN A WHOLE RELATIONSHIP WITH ANOTHER WOMAN THAT'S NOT ME!" She yelled.

There was nothing I could say. She said she never wanted to speak to me again and hung up on me. It took a long time for Tiana to trust me again, but she forgave me, and we moved on.

One year flew by and I was still basking in my happiness. Things were still smooth sailing for me. Tiana and I were still lovers and best friends. While we were cuddling on the couch watching T.V., I heard the voice of God so clearly say to me,

"SHIFT THE RELATIONSHIP."

Totally disturbed by the words spoken to me, I went to the bathroom to regroup. Walking back to the living room, I tried to act normal, but God killed the vibe.

Later that evening, I sat on the bed hesitantly and had a conversation with Tiana about our relationship.

"I don't think we are supposed to be together. Do you think we will go to hell?"

I could not bear looking at the tears in her eyes and hearing her say she did not want to let go. She told me how much she loved me, our family, and how happy she is. After hearing that, I could not let the relationship end. I knew exactly how she was feeling because I loved her equally. We started going to church, praying together, and paying our tithes. I figured God would accept that. I thought He knew my heart and would honor what made me happy. Privately, I prayed that God would change her heart one day to break up with me because I was not going to mention it again. Other than that, we would ride until the wheels fell off.

As time passed, Tiana and I became best friends and "couple goals" of our friends, associates, and anyone we encountered. We loved, honored, cherished, and respected one another. Sending loving emails daily and going

on dates once a week

was our routine. Our

> Everything I ever desired or wanted in a male, I had in Tiana.

date nights were competitive. I had to top everything she did and vice

versa. Anytime we had a break from the kids, we took a road trip. Our

relationship was so dope, Tiana and I dressed alike most days.

Everything I ever desired or wanted in a male, I had in Tiana. I fell

deeper in love daily. The love I had for her compared to no other. I

was prepared to spend the rest of my life with Tiana without question.

She had every piece of me, and I trusted her with my heart and soul.

Our relationship was the best thing that had ever happened to me. I

could not imagine my life outside of her. She was the missing piece

from my life.

Our very first Christmas together, Tiana surprised me with tickets

to see my favorite musical artist, Tamar Braxton, and a stunning

diamond ring. It glistened so beautifully in the sun. She took my

breath away and made my heart skip a couple beats. I was completely

blown away and I said yes without hesitation. That was the best

Christmas, and the smile I wore could not be taken away by any

means. Flipping the script, I secretly planned a romantic dinner for her in our dining room. Tiana was in our room getting dressed under the impression that we were going out to dinner. When she came out of the room she was stunned, looking at the candles tracing around the edges of the table and rose petals scattered across the dining room table and floor.

"Surprise!" I shouted.

After we finished eating dinner, I served her a slice of strawberry cake. While she was eating the cake, she was thrown off guard by the bling that sparkled inside of her cake.

"What is inside my cake!" she said blushing. I was tickled.

"You're not the only one with tricks." We embraced and celebrated the rest of the night.

Over the years, Tiana and I were so in tune with one another we were

> Smoking weed shifted to a daily pattern for me. I was high as a kite every day.

finishing each other's sentences and picking up on each other's habits. I loved to drink wine and alcohol occasionally and Tiana loved to smoke weed. Eventually I started smoking weed just as much as I had wine or an alcoholic beverage. Smoking weed shifted to a daily pattern for me. I was high as a kite every day. Sometimes I would come home on my lunch break and get high. On weekends, I was the wildest. From Friday night until Sunday morning, my system was filled with alcohol and weed.

I threw a fish fry on a Friday night and invited my closest friends, Pamela, and Maria. Pamela, "Pea" was the type of friend that was down for whatever and had absolutely no filter. Her favorite word was "Ninja". Maria was very laid back, loved to joke around, drink, and get high. Anytime we all linked together, it was wild! While I was battering the fish, Pamela knocked at the door.

"IT'S OPEN!" I yelled.

She walked in with grocery bags.

"What's up Pea? I asked you to bring liquor. Tell me why you got groceries?"

She pulled out two bottles of liquor and sarcastically shouted,

"Ninja don't come for me! And the only fish I eat is Swai."

I started laughing when she put a bag of grits on the counter.

"Why do you have grits Pea?" I asked.

"Whatchu mean!? Fish and grits Ninja! You want me to help you cook?" she asked.

"Nah, just make us some drinks."

Minutes later, Maria walks in dancing to the music and shouting, "AYEEE! SHOT TIME!" Y'all ready to Turn up or what?!"

Maria poured a shot for herself, Pea, Tiana, and me. We held up a toast to the "SQUAD". Maria grabbed a deck of cards and sat down at the table.

"Let's get this spade game going," said Maria.

As we were drinking and playing spades, Tiana lit two blunts. Maria pulled four sacks of weed out of her purse.

"Oh, you know I gotta put two more in rotation." WHAM! I smacked an ace of spades down on the table. "Run me my book!" WHAM! "And run me the next one."

Pea played a card from her hand. "Damn, Y'all! Ninjas get aggressive when they get *one* good hand."

We all laughed. Maria pulls out another bag,

"Y'all ready for a bean?" she asked us.

"A what?" I asked.

"A bean! Which one do you want? Dollar Bill, Dice, Incredible Hulk, Joker, Superman?"

Tiana reached and grabbed the Dollar Bill. I had never seen ecstasy pills before, nor was I aware they made them into different characters and shapes. I looked in the bag cautiously asking,

"Am I going to die if I take this?"

"NO!" Maria, Tiana, and Pea said in unison.

"Ok, I'll try the dice."

Maria grabbed the shot glasses and said, "Now let's take another shot."

BAM! BAM! BAM! Someone was banging on the door. Pea looked up, "Y'all know I don't like fake people. Who else y'all invite?"

I opened the door. "Sisterrr!" Shanelle screamed as she walked in.

"Wow! Y'all turning up and didn't invite me? Y'all so fake."

Tiana lit another blunt. "You know I got you," she told Shanelle. Pea poured another round of shots.

"Y'all, we gotta take a shot with my ride or die!" said Pea.

After a while, I didn't know if I was high, drunk or floating. I laughed uncontrollably all night throughout the night, and everything I ate tasted amazing. The grits were so flavorful, and I do not like grits. My eyes were still wide open at 4 a.m. I did not remember anything after blunt number six and shot number seven aside from waking up Saturday afternoon.

Later, that Saturday night after Tiana and I finished eating, we started thinking of places to go. Tiana jumped up in excitement saying,

"Ouu! Let's go to the casino! Something's telling me we're going to win tonight!" I burst into laughter.

"Man, you always say that! And we leave the casino broke every time," I said.

"I'm serious this time. Let's bet $50," said Tiana.

After getting dressed, we stopped by the Circle K gas station to get two cups of ice.

"We're on Remy straight tonight with no chaser!" Tiana hollered, pouring Remy in our cups.

"Why do you gotta be ghetto in public every time we go somewhere?" We both laughed. Tiana rolled three blunts before we drove off. We spent the whole ride to the casino drinking, smoking, and blasting trap music.

When Tiana and I got inside the casino, she looked at me and said, "Pick a machine." The cigarette smell was so strong, I started breathing under the collar of my shirt.

"We gotta get out the cig section first."

In the non-smoking section, I picked a random machine called "Double Devil". I am cheap, so I kept bidding $.25 cents.

"Man, you gotta bid higher than that!" Tiana exclaimed as she bid $1.

"Put yo hands down girl! You gon' get us robbed!"

"See, you're always trying to play like the rich people. That's why we leave broke in twenty minutes," I said. Seconds later, the machine lights started flashing and making loud sounds like a police siren. I looked down and we had 33 free spins with a bonus amount at $230! The money amount continued to increase after every spin.

"AYEEE, WE GETTIN RICH!" I yelled waving my hands in the air.

"PUT YO HANDS DOWN GIRL! YOU GON' GET US ROBBED!" Tiana slapped my hands out of the air. "You gotta hush and act regular," she whispered.

We sat there kicking each other under the chair and squeezing each other's hand in excitement as we tried to keep quiet watching the amount increase to $800. Holding out her hand, Tiana said "I told you we were gonna hit the jackpot! Run me my $50 cash please."

My birthday was approaching, and I was super upbeat and jubilant to see all the surprises Tiana had lined up for me. Every year we would always celebrate the full week leading up to the actual day of our birthdays. On Monday morning I woke up joyous expecting some sort of surprise. Morning, Noon, and evening passed, and I did not receive anything nor did Tiana mention anything. By the time I got off work, my entire mood shifted, and I tried so hard to act normal and not show my saltiness. Tiana came into the kitchen while I was preparing dinner.

"Babe, you've been quiet ever since you got home from work. What's up with you?"

"Nothing. I'm cool." I said trying to hide my irritation. She walked away laughing. The doorbell rang.

"Get the door!" Tiana yells. When I opened the door, there was a delivery guy standing there with a box of edible arrangements and six happy birthday balloons.

"Are you Tamika Ingram?" I stood there in amazement. "Yes, I am." As I closed the door behind me, Tiana was standing there holding a huge bag.

"HAPPY PRE-BIRTHDAY SURPRISE #1!" she said excitedly.

My stomach felt like thousands of butterflies fluttering. I jumped into her arms shouting, "Thank You babe! I thought you forgot!"

"I knew that's why you had a little attitude," she said. While I was sitting in the middle of the floor opening my bag, I fell out and started screaming, "OH MY GOD! THESE ARE THE SNEAKERS I WANTED!" I danced all night on cloud nine.

Tuesday, I received 10 tubes of Mac lipstick. Wednesday was a delivery of six pair of heels. Thursday, she surprised me with four of my favorite perfumes. Friday, I woke up to breakfast in bed. Saturday was the day of my birthday. At midnight, Lamar and Nicole ran and jumped on me with gifts in their hands screaming, "Happy Birthday!" That was the best feeling in the world.

I woke up that morning cheerful and everyone needed to know it was my birthday. "It's My birthday! I repeated over and over. I called my sister waking her from her sleep.

"Girl! It's my birthday and I got Barz! Listen, it's my birthday and I got time to play. Burger King said I can have it my way. I'm turning up all day no matter what people say!"

She burst into laughter, "Mika! Happy Birthday. Please stop rapping man, I'm begging you!"

Tiana took me to breakfast, and afterwards she took me on a long ride. As we passed trees and horses, I started wrecking my brain trying to figure out where in the world she was taking me.

"Where are we going?" I asked.

She handed me a blindfold. "Here, put this on. We are almost there." When we pulled up and got out of the car, I was trying to listen for sounds to determine where we were, but everything was so quiet. She removed the blindfold when we got to the entrance.

"HAPPY BIRTHDAY! Welcome to Brookstone's Winery." Winetasting! Really! Being at a winery for the first time was the best memory in the world. I got a chance to view the vineyard, see how they crush wine, how they store wine and most of all I had the privilege of tasting all sorts of wines. Before, we left the entire staff and all the visitors sang, "Happy Birthday" to me. After tasting nine different types of wine, I was toasted. I had a whole music concert when we got back to the car.

"AYEEEE TURN THAT UP BABE! THAT IS MY JAM!" I sang. We rode for like 2 more hours. *Where are we going now?* I wondered. Eventually we pulled up to Phipps Plaza in Atlanta Ga. "Shopping Spree-ee!" I said, dancing to the door. Tiana handed me the blindfold.

"Here, put these on again. HAPPY BIRTHDAY!" My knees buckled and I could not speak. "That's Rasheeda!" For so long, I wanted to go shopping at her store. Not only was I able to shop, I met her, and we took pictures together. At this moment I was feeling like a VIP! I walked around the whole mall with shades on because I felt too hot for people to see me.

"One last surprise for tonight. The finale!" Tiana exclaimed.

"Where are we going now!" I asked.

"Just chill and ride," she said.

Pulling up to the location she handed me the blindfold again. She walked me all the way inside and removed the blindfold. My body lost feeling and I almost hit the floor. I was at my favorite hangout spot. Trina

We started planning our wedding and setting a date for our ceremony.

Braxton's restaurant *Bar Chix*. I had the pleasure of meeting Trina and Towanda Braxton and I sang with them all night long. We danced and made several videos together. They were officially my sisters. My name changed to Tamika Braxton in my mind ever since that night. I looked at Tiana with googly eyes giving her thousands of kisses.

"Let's plan our wedding, because you did that! This is the best— *EVER!*"

Three years in and my relationship with Tiana was blossoming like a garden of roses. We started planning our wedding and setting a date for our ceremony. Everything seemed perfect, but things weren't. We had switched church memberships to *World Changers* with Pastor Creflo Dollar and got into our Bibles more, but we were getting into arguments every single day. There were days we would not speak, hug, nor have any intimacy at all. We started getting tired of one another and it lasted for months. I loved Tiana, but she didn't know I still kept in touch with Michael on a regular basis. Life was a struggle for me emotionally. The vibes in the house were distant and the kids no longer wanted to be around us because the arguing was constant. My heart could not take the silence another day.

"Tiana, we need to talk. What happened to us?"

"I don't know. We just don't get along anymore, and it seems like we are growing apart."

She was right. I struggled with the idea of being with a woman and not a man. Michael and I still talked a lot, and there was a lot of hurt and unresolved issues between us. I didn't love him anymore, but I thought about going back to him for convenience and for him to be a father to Lamar. Lamar still asked about him often. I also knew being with Tiana was wrong, but I wrestled with letting her go. My life was such a hot mess!

After hours of talking, we decided to make it work and get back to our happy place. Things started getting back on track the more we took trips and spent time together. We started to laugh again, things went back to normal for a long time, and we picked back up on our wedding plans.

About five months later, it was time for me to plan Tiana's birthday. I decided to surprise her with a cruise to the Bahamas. She was in love with the idea of going on a cruise together. We went shopping, buying outfits, new luggage and preparing for our trip. The week before we left to celebrate, I started conversing with Tiana about the different excursions we could pick while on the cruise.

"Ouu babe, you wanna go snorkeling or do you want to swim with the dolphins?" She had a sad demeanor; her responses were dry, and she wasn't engaged the way I expected her to be.

"What's wrong sweetheart?"

Tiana looked at me in tears, "I don't want to be gay anymore."

Seven: Tug of War

Tiana began talking to me and explaining what made her come to that conclusion. I respected her decision completely because I knew that was God. We decided to break up and go on the cruise together as friends. God completely threw a monkey wrench in my plans because I had so many romantic events and reservations set in place. Thinking about all the wonderful things I planned, I just had to get it off my chest.

I said, "I respect us breaking up and all, but can we break up *after* the cruise? You have no idea of the things I planned!"

We both laughed. Now that Tiana no longer wanted to be gay, she wanted to change her style too. We went shopping together to take all her clothes back to the store and exchanged them for feminine clothes and accessories. Shopping together was exciting and new. Watching her try on dresses, swimsuits and skirts was hilarious and enjoyable. While she was in the dressing room, I brought her some booty shorts to try on.

"Let me see how these look on you," I said jokingly. She came out of the dressing room with a distasteful look. "Girl, those are cute! Stick out ya butt!" Tiana and I shopped for hours until we nailed every outfit.

Friday morning had finally come for us to set sail. Photographers met us as soon as we boarded the ship. The view was marvelous. There were elegant glass spiral staircases leading up to the top deck. I was captivated by the huge glass LED crystal chandelier hanging high above the stairs. It has a height of 22 feet, changes color in different variations, and spans vertically to three decks. The design was of spiraling oval discs with hundreds of crystal encrusted balls orbiting around the main structure. Our room had a stunning balcony ocean view. The navy-blue waters were glistening in the sun and blowing with the wind creating the most peaceful sound.

After Tiana and I unpacked our bags, we changed into our swimwear and went to the outside bar on the top floor of the ship. While we were sitting at the bar talking and waiting for the bartender to take our order, a guy came over and asked, "Are y'all sisters?" That was an awkward moment because I was used to being asked, "Is that your girl?" We smiled and said, "No, we're friends."

Hearing myself say that for the first time felt bittersweet. I was happy to be free from the relationship, but I was still in love. Surrounded by hundreds of men and women talking loudly, singing and dancing, I joined in to shift from negative thinking.

A couple of hours later we decided to grab a bite to eat oceanside along the waterfront. The moment I looked into Tiana's eyes my emotions started rumbling in my stomach. I pushed my plate over to the side because I no longer had an appetite.

"What's wrong?" Tiana asked in concern.

"I'm just not hungry," I responded.

"You were just excited to eat less than ten minutes ago. What changed?"

Trying to gather my words, I responded, "I don't know. I just, I miss being under you and being affectionate. Here we are on this cruise together and I can't even kiss you."

Tiana dropped her head in disappointment.

"I know, I've been trying not to think about it since we got here." After much talking, we decided to have fun and make the best out of a difficult situation.

Later that evening, Tiana and I were lying poolside relaxing when the DJ got on the microphone and announced a twerking contest. Twerking is dancing in a sexually provocative manner involving thrusting hip movements and a low squatting stance. To simplify, according to the Urban Dictionary, twerking means to shake your booty up and down. I've never been the one to dance, but I had five shots and four *Sex on the Beach* alcoholic beverages in my system. My mind told me to enter the contest.

"Tiana, I'm about to go twerk!" I said anxiously. She looked at me in disbelief asking, "Are you for real?"

"Yup! Watch me," I said putting my drink down. There were eight other women that entered the twerk contest. Each contestant had to introduce themselves by saying their name and where they were from.

My turn came to introduce myself. I lied about my name and where I was from. I wanted everyone to think I was from outside of the U.S.

"Hi Everybody, my name is Nicole, and I'm from Germany." I said wearing the biggest smile. Every contestant had to give a 60 second lap dance to one of the judges. There were 12 male judges sitting along the deck. Two women almost got into a fight because one woman gave a lap dance to the other woman's husband. When it was my turn, all the men were shouting out at me to come dance on them. Tiana looked at me without saying a word, she pointed to her lap. I knew the men weren't going to vote for me to win because I wasn't dancing for them, so my plans were to give her the best 60 second lap dance she'd ever experienced for the last time. I danced so well Tiana was totally baffled.

"That's how you dance when we break up huh?"

I chuckled, "I had to blow your mind one last time." After the contest, we started walking back to our rooms to get ready for dinner. Tiana and I got off the elevator and she saw the casino.

"Don't even think about it," I said grabbing her hand to pull her in the opposite direction.

The next morning, Tiana and I went out into town to shop and experience different eateries off the ship. The moment we stepped foot in the mall, her eyes went straight to the casino. Before she could get a word out, I already knew what she was about to say.

"OMG YES! Let's go play!"

We had a blast winning $700. Tiana and I stayed out all day until time to head back to the ship. We stayed in the Bahamas for three days and three nights in total bliss.

When we got home it was on and

> I started conversing with a guy named Robert.

poppin' like popcorn. Tiana and I were getting along well for six months solid. We were so amped up at our progress, we decided to make a YouTube Channel entitled, *"Transparency and Truth"*, to tell the world our story and encourage others. After the third video release, all hell broke loose. I started conversing with a guy named Robert. As soon as I told Tiana about him, our arguments intensified daily, and we couldn't be around one another at all. She told me she felt like she no longer mattered to me and that became strenuous for me because I could not console her or anything. All I could do was talk to her and reassure her that I would never turn my back on her. Deep down inside, I wanted to hold her, love on her and comfort her, but I couldn't. One night I was outside sitting in my truck talking on the phone with Robert. I was fully engaged in the conversation until Tiana came downstairs and saw me on the phone. From that point on, every word Robert said was gibberish in my ears. Closing my eyes tight, I whispered to myself, "Please don't come over here. Please don't come over here." Suddenly, I heard three knocks at my window. I opened my eyes and muted the phone.

"Yeah what's up?" I asked as if I didn't know.

Tiana looked at me with her hand on her chin. "You didn't see me calling you? So, who are you on the phone with?"

I felt like she knew the answer already so lying was not going to be in my best interest. "Huh" I responded afraid to say Robert's name.

"*WHO* are you on the phone with!" Tiana screamed.

"Robert, I'll call you back." I got out of the car. "That was Robert." Tiana knocked the phone out of my hand and went bananas.

"YOU'RE JUST GOING TO KEEP TALKING TO THE NIGGA IN MY DAMN FACE! THAT'S SOME FOUL SHIT! DON'T EVER TALK TO ME AND THAT'S ON MY LIFE. I MEAN THAT!"

She got in her car and sped off. I was angry, hurt and confused. We aren't together, but it seems like I'm wrong for trying to move forward when I'm really not. My mind and emotions were all over the place.

Tiana came back late that night giving me the silent treatment. After I showered, I climbed in bed with her and held her close to me. She broke like glass and I could feel her body breaking down in my arms as she cried. "This is hard! This is my life and I'm watching you move on. I just love you so much."

Hearing her break down crushed my entire soul. "I *haven't* moved on. I'm just trying to move forward somehow. Please stop crying." I began kissing her forehead while holding her tight.

"It feels like you don't love me anymore," she said.

"That's not fair. I'm still in love with you Tiana. You are so mean to me and that hurts. What do you want me to do?" Without thinking, I kissed her lips and made love to her.

The next three days, I found myself treating Tiana like we were in a relationship again. We were intimate, laughing and being in each other's space like old times. She was happy and that's all that mattered to me. One evening, I had a dream that showed me if I stayed in the relationship we would drown and never make it out, but if I let her go, we would be okay. After Tiana finished cutting hair, I told her that we needed to talk.

"I love you, but we can't keep doing this. We have to move forward and push through this pain somehow."

Tiana nodded. "You're right. I was thinking the same thing."

We talked things out and set a date in concrete to move out from one another. Anytime we felt weak, we prayed, talked it out or gave each other space.

Sunday morning Tiana and I drove to Atlanta for church. The service was dynamite, and we ended up dedicating our lives back to God, getting filled with the Holy Spirit with having the evidence of speaking in tongues. I also decided to get baptized again to start my life over fresh and new. Walking back to the car Tiana was so excited that she spoke in tongues for the first time.

"Lemme hear you speak in tongues girl!"

"NOOO!" She said. I was so tickled. I haven't spoken in tongues since I was like 14 or 15 years old. The whole ride home Tiana was on the passenger side practicing her tongues, "Sha-la-la- boe-sha"! She had me laughing so hard I almost swerved off the road.

The entire week all we did was pack and throw away things we no longer wanted. As I was going through some of my things from our relationship, I struggled to toss them in the trash can. Reading the birthday cards and all the letters I kept over the years had me in an extremely low spirit. The more I came across things I immediately threw them away without opening them to avoid my emotions taking over. Day by day, our apartment was getting emptier. The night before we moved out, reality sat in and we embraced one another. The tears started to fall as we shared our feelings towards one another and vowed to stick it out for the Glory of God. The longer we held each other, the more we cried. That was our last night together. We knew everything was about to change and our lives together were over.

Eight: Face Her

On the morning of May 30, 2019, I began Moving into my new apartment. It was so hot outside that you could see the heat waves. Moving was stressful and draining because we moved the hood way. The crew consisted of, "The Homies." Our homies told another homie and they invited their homies. My version of a U-Haul were cars, an SUV and a pickup truck. There were at least 6 vehicles in the lineup following one another to my new apartment like we were driving to a funeral. It took all day to move and we made at least 40 trips up and down the stairs. I will never move on the second floor again. Going up and down those stairs was exhausting.

When we finally finished moving everything, I was ecstatic to be in my new apartment until I looked up and saw those antique looking chandeliers in the living room and dining room.

"Those don't look like the chandeliers the property manager showed me in the model apartment," I said. After I walked through the apartment to check everything else, I called the main office. "Thank you for calling Liberty Place Properties. I'm Alex, how may I help you today?".

"Hey, I'm Tamika Ingram. I just moved to C-6 today and these chandeliers look B.C. like Jesus came and left them over 2,000 years ago. Will you please replace them with a more modern version?"

"I believe those chandeliers are new Ms. Ingram."

"Negative, "I said shaking my head. "They're the total opposite of the chandeliers I saw in the model apartment."
Alex placed me on hold for a couple minutes. When he came back to the phone, he told me a work order was put in for new chandeliers and maintenance would install them as soon as they were delivered.

I started unpacking dishes and putting them in the cabinet. My phone started flashing letting me know I had a text message. Looking down at my phone, I saw a message from Tiana that said, *"I'm just letting you know we made it home. Take care and I look forward to linking up soon. Later."* Tiana and I made an agreement to remain distant and cut off all communication between us for a while. I needed to find myself outside of her and time apart to shift from loving her to just being a friend so we could be effective in ministry together. It hit me after I read the text message, that my life was about to change drastically, and my old way of living was now dead. The thought of change brought tears to my eyes.

> Breaking up for God was more challenging than I thought.

The feeling was new without Tiana and Nicole. Sitting on the couch, I started scrolling through pictures and videos on my phone. Looking back on all the memories we created as a couple and as a family had me reminiscing, laughing, and crying all at the same time. For three years, my life consisted of the four of us every day. Now, I had to sleep in my own bed with no one else in it. I had to go from talking to the one person I shared everything with to absolutely no communication for however long. Breaking up for God was more challenging than I thought. Sometimes I wish we ended on bad terms, because it would have made it easier to get over her. This process was not easy to adjust to overnight. Embracing change was difficult for me.

Every morning I would wake up listening to sermons and gospel music to shift my mind on positivity. No matter how many sermons I listened to, my mind still veered to my old way of life. I started working out more and spending more time with Lamar. My days were so busy, by the time I came home it was time to go to bed. Feeling restless every day, I told myself there had to be a better way to manage. Sunday morning came and I decided to visit a church for a local membership. There was a church called, "Kingdom Living Ministries." I loved the service and after visiting a couple Sundays, I decided to stay and assist the Pastor in pushing her ministry. Over the course of time, the Pastor added me to the minister's group. She later called me back and told me she removed me because the other ministers were complaining that I was a part of leadership faster than they were. Even though I felt wronged, I still stayed.

One Sunday I was asked to teach Sunday School. I was super nervous, but I did not want to be disobedient, so I obliged. The entire week I prayed, studied, and took notes. Sunday came for me to teach Sunday School. I opened in prayer and began to teach the lesson provided. "God is loving, he does not want us to judge or condemn anyone. We should love his people no matter what they look like."

"I'M NOT ABOUT TO WATER DOWN THE WORD OF GOD FOR ANYBODY!" One of the ministers stood up and said arrogantly.

"THAT'S RIGHT!" one of the deacons agreed.

"IF YOU BOLD ENOUGH TO COME TO CHURCH WRONG, BE BOLD ENOUGH TO GET CORRECTED," one of the audio guys said. Almost every church member stood up and said something against what I spoke. They started being ignorant, passing around the collection basket and more. The rest of the Sunday School lesson was taken over by the church members. I never returned.

The following Sunday I decided to visit a different church and felt welcomed instantly. The presence of God was in the atmosphere and I loved every moment of service. Being there inspired me to start working on myself and helped me to dig within myself to help others. I started to read more, pray more, and my days were better the more I stayed focused on positivity and in the Word of God. Embracing my new life started to feel amazingly awesome. After a couple of weeks, I started making inspirational videos to encourage others. Seemingly, I was completely happy until one day I just wasn't in the mood to inspire anyone. I was unable to shake the feeling, and I couldn't give God my all anymore. The thoughts of what happened at the previous church kept resurfacing in my mind. That situation really hurt internally, and I started feeling empty inside. My self-esteem was shot. Anger started rising inside of me. Who I was projecting to be wasn't matching who I was internally, and I knew there had to be a deeper root cause. Even though Tiana and I broke up and I was trying to pick up the pieces in my life, there were several things I still needed to face.

To get to the substratum of everything that shaped my character, I had to face it by going back to the root of where it started. I needed to be completely naked and honest with myself about it all. I no longer wanted insecurity, anger, low self-esteem and unforgiveness to have control and continue to follow me. It was time for me to take full responsibility for my behavior and decisions. I have been running long enough and there is nowhere else to run besides the mirror.

The underlying emotion of insecurity was overwhelmingly shaping my self-image and influencing my behavior. It's so easy to cover up insecurity with smiles, laughter, a relationship, accomplishments, etc. but it's hard to keep it covered. My insecurities started presenting themselves in my relationships. Growing up, I've never seen a healthy marriage. I was unaware of whether I was valuable to my parents. My mother missed every track meet, soccer game, drill meet, cheerleading competition, and theatre show, but she was always available when the church wanted her. Her not being there to support my activities birthed forth rejection. I always wanted to be accepted by someone. My dad wasn't sensitive to my feelings. He always talked with force, put me down or cursed me out which birthed forth anger.

Insecurity is uncertainty about oneself or lack of confidence. I stayed with guys that just wanted sex. I stayed in an abusive marriage and I decided to be with women MAINLY because I was uncertain of myself. Being uncertain of who I was, caused me to accept and tolerate things that hurt me. I knew I was worth being treated right, but I wasn't confident in my worth. The confidence I needed to have in myself before I started engaging in relationships wasn't there the way I thought it was. I was often uncertain if a man would really love, honor, and cherish me, and this caused me to stay trapped with a woman for as long as I could. Uncertainty makes people afraid. I never stood up for myself because I didn't want the people that mattered to walk away from me.

Anger was the number one emotion I suffered from. When I got angry, no one could convince me that I didn't have a right to be angry. There was always a justification for my anger, and I had no respect for the person who caused me to be angry. Whenever someone said something to me, I didn't like, I would curse them out so bad they wanted to fight me. Lashing out in anger caused me to say things that would hurt the individual. It is true that hurt people hurt people. My trigger buttons were off limits. There were certain areas that automatically triggered anger. I blamed my behavior on anyone that upset me. Anger is the strong emotion that you feel when you think that someone has behaved in an unfair, cruel, or unacceptable way. I spent over half of my life with a short fuse like a firecracker. Have you ever been so angry that you cried? I've cried hundreds of times from being angry and I didn't know it's because anger stems from hurt. Anger is the secondhand emotion that manifests pain. Anger distracts people from the suppressed hurt from pain and causes them to focus completely on the person or thing that triggered the anger. It's the trigger area I needed to address the most, because when anger was the focus, it hid the pain that was rooted on the inside of me. Where was this pain coming from? What really caused me to snap and lash out towards others?

My temper was based on pain that started when I was a little girl. I have been through some rough times in my life, and for many years those experiences caused me to feel miserable. I harbored hurt and disappointment most of my life. Anger was easily triggered because I had been hurt by the people I loved, respected, or positioned first class in my life. My dad hurt me to the core. He was "superior" in my world. In my eyes, my dad would never do anything to cause harm, hurt or damage. All the times he put me down, cursed me out and betrayed me, and crushed my spirit, I felt disowned and rejected. Anger automatically stood up anytime someone said something that prompted me to feel rejected, degraded, unloved or taken advantage of. There was no way I was going to allow anybody to step over me again.

They say, "Never Judge A Book by Its Cover." I'm 5'6, butter pecan tan with honey blonde hair, a slim waist, beautiful brown eyes, toned thighs, and a bright smile that illuminates any dark room. Fashion and working out are my pastimes. Therefore, I always dress stylish and classy. With all these beautiful attributes, I still struggled with low self-esteem. My outer beauty wasn't equivalent to the way I viewed myself internally. Getting pregnant at nineteen years old took a toll on my self-esteem and it only got worse over the years. Men would always say how beautiful, gorgeous, and amazing I was, yet they cheated, abused me, and viewed me only as a snack. According to the Urban Dictionary, a snack is defined as, "A person with a good body/face." Guys always made me feel like sex came with the territory of being their woman. Everything they asked of me, I did to feel accepted. Instead of making wiser decisions, I blamed the individual that hurt me. Every time someone said something negative about me, I always ran to my mom or my friends for reassurance. I always sought validation from others to feel good about who I was. It was hard to admit to myself that I had low self-esteem.

For years, I convinced myself I was over my past yet every time something reminded me of it, I lashed out. Looking at people that hurt me or being in their space made my body cringe, and if I could avoid them altogether, I did. Admitting to myself that I still had unforgiveness in my heart was a fight. I realized my anger came from unforgiveness as well. There were so many emotions I had to address.

Dealing with myself was hard work. The first person I needed to forgive was me. Most people don't want to deal with themselves, but I had no choice. The only way I live forever in total bliss and see the manifestation of all God has for me is to give up everything that's suffocating my destiny. I was okay with giving up some things in my life but to give up everything was a stretch. Those sensitive, hurtful, and weak areas were much easier to hold on to and suppress deep down inside. The way I lived my life became comfortable, but deep down inside I was slowly dying from unhappiness. If I did not kill everything in my past, they would continue to speak in my future.

Nine: Flatline

Choosing to kill the person I loved the most was a difficult decision. I had been leaning and depending on her for over half of my life. The first thing I needed was help, because there was no way I could take her out in my own strength. I had to abandon her entirely and **SURRENDER** to God. *To surrender is (1) to cease resistance; (2) abandon oneself entirely.* God would not force Himself into my life, because He is a gentleman and allows me to make my own choices. Kneeling and raising my hands as a sign of surrender, I prayed,

"Lord, I am in desperate need of you. I give up my ways for your ways. I give up my thoughts in exchange for your thoughts and my understanding for your wisdom. Come into my heart and change my desires for your desires. Help me to see what you created in me. Give me the strength to overcome every obstacle in my path. I cannot do this without your help, because in you I am strong. I surrender emotional soul-ties, bitterness, anger, low self-esteem, lesbianism, impatience, hurt and fear. Have your way in me. In Jesus name, Amen."

After surrendering, I had to go back and put her to death using the power and authority that I possess. My mind was made up to devour her, leaving no traceable evidence. To devour her, I had to outthink her, so I came up with a D.E.A.T.H. plan.

D - <u>Destroy Negative Thoughts.</u> **Destroy** means *to put an end to the existence of something by attacking it.* My mouth is the most powerful tool to attack her thoughts. Every time a negative thought entered her mind; I spoke positively against it.

E - <u>Eliminate Distractions</u>- "Don't Bite the Bait!" **Eliminate** *means to get rid of.* This is when the fight became intense because I disconnected her from certain people, and certain activities.

A - <u>Accept Your Authority</u> - **Accept** means *to receive and believe.* I revoked her access to make decisions and take on full ownership of every move made going forward.

T - <u>Take Total Control-</u> **Control** means *the power to direct.* I dictate her life completely making her body a slave to my commands.

H - <u>Have Keen Vision.</u> Her ability to see led to destruction, so I shut off her eyesight to have a **sharp vision** for my future.

D - <u>Destroy Negative Thoughts.</u> Negative thoughts are toxic and a major hindrance that was blocking my ability to move forward. I tried going to church, listening to sermons on YouTube, and reading the Bible and I still failed. Hearing other preachers was just motivational. Reading the Bible is inspiring, but it is only life-changing when applied. It was not until I realized that the most powerful tool I possess is my mouth. Nothing changed in my life until I started to apply everything I heard and read by opening my own mouth. Regardless of what I feel and what I am facing, I can change it if I believe what I speak. The Bible says in Romans 12:2, *be transformed by the renewing of your mind.* It also says in Proverbs 23:7, *So as a man thinketh, so is he.* Wait, so whatever I ponder on, that is what I am? After reading that, the lightbulb went off. I always thought I was a failure and that I was not good enough. That is why I settled my whole life! I transformed my mind quick because one thing I am not—is a failure. I had to consistently say, "I AM NOT A FAILURE!" even when it seemed like failure. At first, it was hard to do because it is hard to think of the good during a bad situation. The bad feels like it rules out any possibility of a positive outcome. One bad situation could create a million negative thoughts that kept influencing me to quit. Intense situations are designed to see if I will speak life or death and I choose life. Every time that a negative thought surfaced, I counteracted it with speaking a positive word. When I heard myself speak it, I started believing what I spoke. When I believed what I spoke, I started lining up to what I spoke, and then I started to see the manifestation of what I spoke. Seeing the manifestation of my words motivates me to keep speaking no matter what I face.

E - Eliminate Distractions. Distractions can seem impossible to avoid. People mostly compare distractions with the inability to focus. I realized that distractions are also associated with identity theft. Every distraction I faced altered who I was because I bit the bait of everything that dangled before me, not sometimes but *every time*. I bit baits of lust, anger, and rejection. When things blew up in my face,

I was somewhere playing the victim and looking crazy. Some fish even know when to swim past the distraction of bait. Why can't I? Truth is because I didn't want to disconnect. I chose to give in to the distractions. Nobody made me do it. The Bible says in Proverbs 4:25, *Let your eyes look straight ahead and fix your gaze directly in front of you.* I wanted to look everywhere but straight, until I got so tired of going around in the same circles, causing misery on myself because I kept letting people in my cookie jar; because I didn't want to let go of people I was attached to and bad habits that distracted me from the real me. I had to say, "Enough is enough." Jeremiah 29:11 says, *I have plans to prosper you not to harm you, plans to give you hope and a future.* You mean to tell me Here I am, 28 years old, and I could have been walking in the promises of God that He already had waiting on me! He just wants me to look straight ahead and recognize the bait that comes from different angles as distractions. Hmph, hmph, hmph....... I was playing myself the whole time. At that moment, I started releasing people I have let stay in my life too long and things I was holding on to that were ultimately detrimental. I felt bad about it initially and it was a struggle to resist but I had to realize my life matters more than distractions. Day after day of keeping my eyes ahead of me, I started smiling again and coming into the bold woman God created me to be with the power to say, "NO" to distractions. I can smell a distraction from a mile away, and where I'm headed, I can't afford it. Deuces!

A - <u>Accept Your Authority.</u> Every trap I fell into was because I let it happen. There were days I did not know if I was coming or going. I stayed stressed out because I just let situations and circumstances consume me, and my brain felt like it was submerged underwater losing oxygen. Sometimes I did not eat because I made my day so busy to avoid dealing with my internal issues. My temper was short and I spazzed quickly on anyone that breathed wrong in my direction. I did not believe, nor did I receive the authority I have on the inside of me to take control over my emotions. Feeling sad and always angry was getting tiresome to my mind. Luke 10:19 says, *I have given you authority to trample on snakes and scorpions and to overcome the power of the enemy; nothing will harm you.* I have the power to give orders, make decisions and enforce obedience. Majority of the time, the weight felt so heavy I just wanted to give up on life completely and say, "To hell with authority! This is too much!" I had to put my foot down and take away her rights to rule over me. I grabbed hold of my thoughts because whatever I think, my emotions will follow. Taking control over my emotions keeps my sanity. I will not sulk in sorrow another night and I absolutely refused to use energy screaming at anyone else. Most importantly, I will not be another victim of suicide. When I feel my emotions rising, I use my authority and speak to them, "SIT DOWN, SHUT UP, SHIFT AND DO IT NOW!" Sometimes I have to repeat it over and over until my mood shifts. I had to fall out of love with my feelings and continue to push through negative emotions. I have the power to feel however I want to feel after seeing the power behind my authority and the ability to maintain my joy when I would have lost it. I work my authority daily, so my emotions are no longer able to have a say in my life.

   T - Take Total Control. I learned that it is important that I take control over every area of my life. The flesh has no power at all, yet it loves to act as boss. Whatever I felt like doing, I did. If I wanted to have sex, I did, If I wanted to curse somebody out, I did. If I wanted to cheat, I did. If I wanted to lie, I did. Having lost all control, I was just letting her run wild living in bondage and controlling every move and decision I made. The Bible says in Proverbs 25:28, *A man without self-control is like a city broken into and left without walls.*

I allowed the people, drama, and unforgiveness to control me. It took total control over how I lived my daily life. I held grudges against people because of what they had done to me. Pretending to be happy got played out and doing whatever I wanted was not beneficial to me. I wanted to be genuinely happy within myself, so I had to take my control back from her and tell her to do what I said. When I saw my dad and stepmother, I forgave them and loved them genuinely. Because I decided to let the hurt go, we are closer than we ever were before, and we can laugh and smile together. I took total control over my body, my mind, and emotions. My purity will remain until marriage. It feels so good to have control and not allow anything or anyone else dictating my life.

H - Have Keen Vision. From the age of 18 up until the age of 28, I had cataract vision. Every decision I made concerning the direction of my life was foggy and unclear. I have had so many wrecks in life and setbacks in life because I made decisions with cataracts over my eyes. What's crazy is, sometimes I was aware that the decisions were dumb and still made them. Hosea 4:6 says *My people perish for the lack of knowledge*. To deliberately make dumb choices and hope something amazing comes from them is insanity. I ran myself ragged until I concluded that I genuinely wanted better for my life and better for my

son. Listening to a million preachers meant nothing until I got tired

of her. John 10:10 says, *The thief comes only to steal, kill, and*

destroy. He does not have the power to kill me, He wants to suggest

things and present things before me so that I will destroy myself. I had

to shut down her eyesight to have keen vision over my own life. Once

I closed her eyes, I started to see things for what they were, I started

moving differently. Things became clearer in my life, and I started to

see what was and what was not for me. Distractions were clear to me.

No longer will I settle for mediocrity when I am destined for the best.

Now I have Hawk Vision. I am watching everything that looks like it

is after my destiny. I am attacking anything that looks like it is

standing in the way.

I have stripped her of all power and control. The final step to

shutting her down completely is to PULL THE PLUG! *POP!* Now,

SHE CAN LIVE for eternity and use the shell of her body to live

through. I have overcome everything the enemy tried to throw that he

thought would kill me. What the enemy meant for bad, God turned it

all around for my good. Going through all the hell and pain made me

stronger, tougher, and smarter. Killing her made me a survivor. Now nothing can stop me from achieving greatness. When I look back over my life and look back at HER......AHH HAAA DEVIL! SHE LIVES! I refuse to be in this world and hand myself over to the enemy as prey to squeeze the life out of me like a python snake, when I am a Queen that holds *POWER* and *AUTHORITY* to trample upon snakes! My spirit is strong, and I am no longer afraid to face the enemy. As storms come, I will soar through them like an eagle. I will no longer run away from my problems but will face them boldly. My confidence is at 100 and I no longer need validation from anyone because God has already validated me. Jeremiah 1:5 boldly states, *Before I formed you in the womb, I knew you, before you were born, I set you apart. I set you apart to be a prophet amongst the nations.* I AM THE CHOSEN ONE! I will keep inspiring and empowering others until my spirit is caught up in heaven.

Old things have passed away and all things are brand new for I am a new creature in Christ Jesus! (2nd Corinthians 5:17) My swag is different, and I view my life totally different. I walk with boogie in my blood because I am superior!

Every decision we make has an outcome that leads to life or death. My question to you is, which will you choose?

"If you try to hang on to your life, you will lose it. But if you give up your life for My sake and for the sake of the Good News, you will save it." -Mark 8:35

Letter to Kings and Queens

Dear Kings and Queens,

You are not defined or obligated to your past! THE OLD YOU IS DEFEATED! You are BETTER, FASTER, and STRONGER than the old you! You are a new creation in Christ Jesus born with a purpose, future, and destiny that only YOU can fulfill. YOU WERE BORN A WINNER! You were born BLESSED! The enemy is intimidated by the POWER AND AUTHORITY that you possess. He is trying to distract you with any and everything to try and break you down. TODAY! We are serving NOTICE on the enemy; HE HAS NO AUTHORITY OVER YOU, YOUR MIND, WILL OR EMOTIONS! Life's obstacles are designed to help develop ENDURANCE so don't get weary in well doing! You have the POWER to not give way to your circumstances. Endurance develops STRENGTH AND CHARACTER! You can withstand all pressure. When the pressure feels heavy, exercise your strength! You have the character of the Most High living on the inside of you. Character builds CONFIDENCE and HOPE of salvation. YOU ARE A CONQUER! YOU ARE NOT WEAK! YOU SHALL LIVE AND NOT DIE! Your purpose is BIGGER and GREATER than your human eyes can see. Eyes haven't seen and ears have not heard the "BIG" God has in store for you.

HOLD YOUR HEAD UP AND LIVE!

Love,

-Tamika Nicole

About the Author

Tamika Ingram was born in Wiesbaden, Germany to parents Lee Gardner and Frances Marshall. Tamika now resides in Columbus, Georgia, where she is a Fitness Coach and Inspirational Speaker transforming the way people think about health and fitness. It is no surprise how Tamika's captivating personality allows her to reach people and encourage them along their life transformations. Her passion for motivating fellow kings and queens to be confident in who they are and regain their smiles is obvious and refreshing. Those who know Tamika, know that instilling confidence starts at home and with Tyler, her 10-year-old son.

Tamika enjoys fashion designing, living a healthy, active lifestyle by exercising and helping people on their journey to knowing Christ. She is committed to being a minister of the gospel and a youth leader at Faith Chapel where she currently worships. Tamika's dramatic, yet down to earth personality is a blessing to those around her, and she strives to make them feel like friends reunited. Tamika's many talents, generosity in ministry, and Life Coaching serve well. Her creativity through her words, style and overall approach to life has established her as the strong, successful overachiever that she is.

Email: tamikaingram26@gmail.com
Facebook: Tamika Nicole
Instagram: Tamikanicolee

About the Publisher

At **the Vision to Fruition Publishing House**, we are dedicated to helping others bring their personal, business, ministry, and other visions to fruition. Whether your vision is a book you want to write, a business you want to start, a conference or event you want to host, a ministry you want to launch or an organization you want to start; or requires a more technical aspect like computer repairs, logo designs or web designs; we can help. **The Vision to Fruition Publishing House** is the publishing branch of **the Vision to Fruition Group**. We will help you walk through the process and set you up for success! At **the Vision to Fruition Group** we have more than just clients, we have *Visionaries*. We provide solutions to equip others to pursue their visions and dreams with reckless abandon. Since 2017, we have published over 30 authors, several of which were Amazon Bestsellers. We would love for you to join our family of Visionaries as well!

Learn more here: **www.vision-fruition.com**

Made in the USA
Columbia, SC
17 August 2020